BLACK LIVES
NATIVE LANDS
WHITE WORLDS

Other Books from Bright Leaf

House Stories
The Meanings of Home in a New England Town
BETH LUEY

Bricklayer Bill
The Untold Story of the Workingman's Boston Marathon
PATRICK L. KENNEDY AND LAWRENCE W. KENNEDY

Concrete Changes
Architecture, Politics, and the Design of Boston City Hall
BRIAN M. SIRMAN

Williamstown and Williams College
Explorations in Local History
DUSTIN GRIFFIN

Massachusetts Treasures
A Guide to Marvelous, Must-See Museums
CHUCK D'IMPERIO

Boston's Twentieth-Century Bicycling Renaissance
Cultural Change on Two Wheels
LORENZ J. FINISON

Went to the Devil
A Yankee Whaler in the Slave Trade
ANTHONY J. CONNORS

At Home
Historic Houses of Eastern Massachusetts
BETH LUEY

At Home
Historic Houses of Central and Western Massachusetts
BETH LUEY

Flight Calls
Exploring Massachusetts through Birds
JOHN R. NELSON

BLACK LIVES
NATIVE LANDS
WHITE WORLDS

A HISTORY OF
SLAVERY
IN NEW ENGLAND

Jared Ross Hardesty

 BRIGHT LEAF
AMHERST AND BOSTON

An imprint of University of Massachusetts Press

Black Lives, Native Lands, White Worlds has been supported by
the Regional Books Fund, established by donors in 2019 to support
the University of Massachusetts Press's Bright Leaf imprint.

Bright Leaf, an imprint of University of Massachusetts Press, publishes accessible and
entertaining books about New England. Highlighting the history, culture, diversity, and
environment of the region, Bright Leaf offers readers the tools and inspiration to explore its
landmarks and traditions, famous personalities, and distinctive flora and fauna.

ISBN 978-1-62534-457-1 (paper); 456-4 (hardcover)

Designed by Sally Nichols
Set in Adobe Calson Pro and Cheltanham
Printed and bound by Maple Press, Inc.
Cover design and art by Thomas Eykemans

Library of Congress Cataloging-in-Publication Data

Names: Hardesty, Jared, author.
Title: Black lives, native lands, white worlds : a history of slavery in
  New England / Jared Ross Hardesty.
Description: Amherst : Bright Leaf, an imprint of University of
  Massachusetts Press, 2019. | Includes bibliographical references and
  index. | Summary: "Shortly after the first Europeans arrived in
  seventeenth-century New England, they began to import Africans and
  capture the area's indigenous peoples as slaves. By the eve of the
  American Revolution, enslaved people comprised only about 4 percent of
  the population, but slavery had become instrumental to the region's
  economy and had shaped its cultural traditions. This story of slavery in
  New England has been little told. In this concise yet comprehensive
  history, Jared Ross Hardesty focuses on the individual stories of
  enslaved people, bringing their experiences to life. He also explores
  larger issues such as the importance of slavery to the colonization of
  the region and to agriculture and industry, New England's deep
  connections to Caribbean plantation societies, and the significance of
  emancipation movements in the era of the American Revolution. Thoroughly
  researched and engagingly written, Black Lives, Native Lands, White
  Worlds is a must-read for anyone interested in the history of New
  England"—Provided by publisher.
Identifiers: LCCN 2019019874 | ISBN 9781625344564 (hardcover) | ISBN
  9781625344571 (paperback) | ISBN 9781613767016 (ebook) | ISBN
  9781613767009 (ebook)
Subjects: LCSH: Slavery—New England—History. | Slaves—New
  England—History. | Indian slaves—New England—History. | New
  England—Race relations. | New England—History—Colonial period, ca.
  1600–1775.
Classification: LCC E445.N5 H37 2019 | DDC 306.3/620974—dc23
LC record available at https://lccn.loc.gov/2019019874

British Library Cataloguing-in-Publication Data
A catalog record for this book is available from the British Library

For Dana

Contents

A Note on the Text, Dates, and Terminology ix

Preface

15 George Street, Medford, Massachusetts 02155 xiii

Acknowledgments xix

CHAPTER 1 ORIGINS   1

CHAPTER 2 TRAFFICKED PEOPLE   25

CHAPTER 3 SLAVE AND SOCIETY   49

CHAPTER 4 WORKING WORLDS   70

CHAPTER 5 KIN AND COMMUNITY   93

CHAPTER 6 REVOLUTION AND EMANCIPATION   118

EPILOGUE THE PROBLEMS OF EMANCIPATION   143

Further Reading 155

Notes 161

Index 171

A Note on the Text, Dates,
and Terminology

This book quotes original documents from the seventeenth, eighteenth, and early nineteenth centuries. In those periods, there was no uniform writing style. Writing was phonetic, meaning authors spelled words the way they sounded. Likewise, punctuation and capitalization were not standardized. To adhere as closely to the documents as possible, the text retains the misspellings, unsystematic capitalization, and erratic punctuation throughout. Superscript abbreviations, such as "ye" for "the," "wch" for "which," or "yr" for "your," however, have been modernized and spelled out in full.

Dates have likewise been modernized. Before September 1752, the British Empire remained on the Julian calendar and celebrated the new year on 25 March. For that reason, the calendar used by the British was twelve days behind the Gregorian calendar used by the rest of Europe. Likewise, dates between 1 January and 24 March were often recorded with both the previous and new year dates. For example, 15 January 1723 would be recorded as "15 January 1722/23." To avoid any confusion, this text uses 1 January as the New Year but does not change the day to conform to the Gregorian calendar. For example, "15 January 1722/23" appears as "15 January 1723."

Finally, terminology can be complicated in a book about slavery. This text interchangeably uses the terms "slave," "bondsmen and women," and "enslaved." The latter, however, is deployed most frequently, especially when emphasizing the agency enslaved men and women attempted to exercise over their own lives. Moreover, given that white colonists in New England enslaved people of indigenous American and African descent, the text utilizes catch-all terms such as "enslaved people" to be as comprehensive as possible, while attempting to be clear about who was enslaved and their racial categorization whenever possible. Likewise, the book uses the term "Indian" because that is the preferred nomenclature of indigenous people still living in the region today. It also deploys the contemporaneous term "people of color" to describe all enslaved and freed people. Nevertheless, when examining the coming of the American Revolution and emancipation, since most activists for abolition and civil rights were of African descent, the terms "free black," "freed black," and "enslaved African" appear.

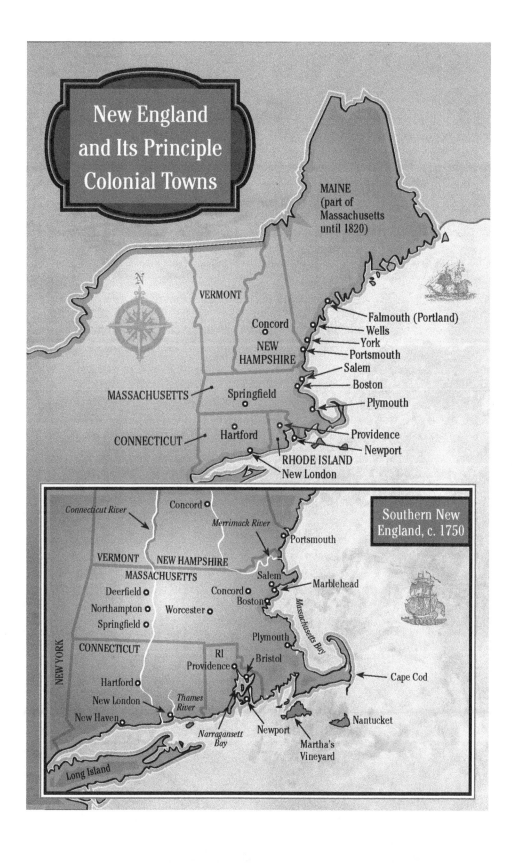

New England
and Its Principle
Colonial Towns

MAINE
(part of
Massachusetts
until 1820)

VERMONT

Concord

NEW
HAMPSHIRE

Falmouth (Portland)
Wells
York
Portsmouth
Salem
Boston
Plymouth

MASSACHUSETTS

Springfield

CONNECTICUT

Hartford

Providence
Newport

RHODE ISLAND
New London

Southern New
England, c. 1750

Connecticut River

Concord

Merrimack River

Portsmouth

VERMONT   NEW HAMPSHIRE
MASSACHUSETTS

Salem
Marblehead

Deerfield

Northampton   Worcester

Concord
Boston

Springfield

Massachusetts Bay

Plymouth

NEW YORK

CONNECTICUT

RI
Providence   Bristol

Cape Cod

Hartford

Thames
River

New London

New Haven

Narragansett
Bay

Newport

Martha's
Vineyard

Nantucket

Long Island

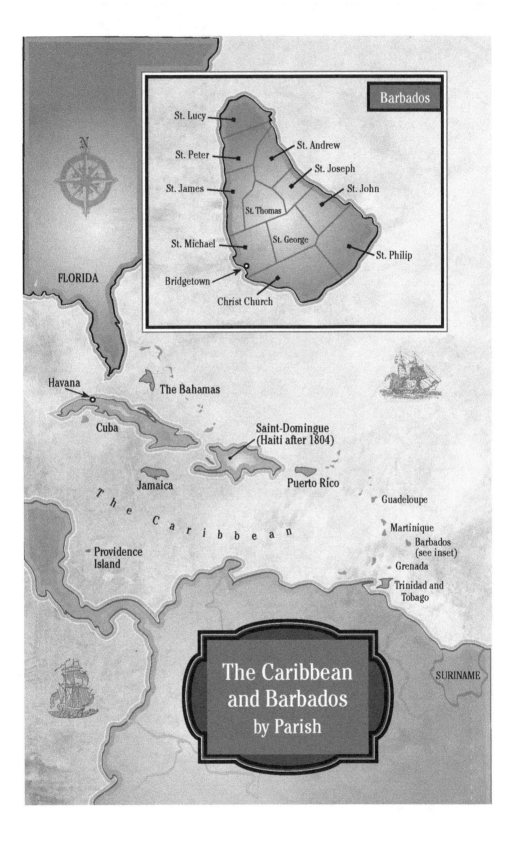

The Caribbean and Barbados by Parish

Preface

Standing in the middle of a modern residential neighborhood in suburban Boston, Massachusetts, is an eighteenth-century Georgian mansion. These are not an uncommon site in New England, a region that embraces its history with placards, tourist attractions, and historic homes. Yet, the house at 15 George Street in Medford stands out—even by New England standards.

Well, not the house specifically but rather the building that stands in front, between the house and George Street. It is unique. Too many windows and not quite large enough to be a barn, its central chimney suggests a different purpose: a dwelling place for people. But why would a mansion, already three stories tall with many bedrooms, require additional living space?

This address was the home of the Royall family. Isaac Royall Sr. purchased the property, which included a two-story dwelling house and five hundred acres of surrounding land in 1732. Over the next five years, he remodeled and added on to the house extensively, transforming it into the mansion that still stands there today. He also had the unusual outbuilding constructed. Upon Isaac Sr.'s death in 1739, the property passed to his son Isaac Royall Jr.

The mansion house gives away much about the man who had it built. Adorned with a golden pineapple doorknocker and surrounded by a wall likewise adorned with pineapples, this home paid homage to the tropics. Although Isaac Sr. was born in Massachusetts, he had spent much of his life in the British West Indian colony of Antigua. There, Royall dealt in sugar, rum, and slaves. Eventually, after a devastating hurricane, pestilence, and a slave conspiracy struck the island, Royall decided to take his family and fortune back to New England.

Royall did not leave all his property behind in Antigua, however. Dwelling in that unusual outbuilding at 15 George Street were many of the twenty-two enslaved men and women Royall brought with him from the Caribbean. That building was a slave quarters. These men and women, most of them born in Africa, were trafficked by Royall to make his new country estate a success. Ripped from their homes for a second time, the people living in that outbuilding worked Royall's farm, kept his house, and took care of his family. And they created a life of their own, demonstrated by the many artifacts they left behind.

The slave quarters standing at 15 George Street is the only freestanding slave quarters north of the Mason-Dixon Line still existing in the United States. Certainly there are many slave quarters in the South and Caribbean, but suburban Boston? This building suggests a different history of New England, one that is not only littered with Puritans and patriots but also enslaved Africans and Indians.

The slave quarters at 15 George Street opens a whole world of slavery in New England. It was deeply connected, culturally, socially, and economically, to slavery in the Caribbean. Enslaved men and women in New England clung to their cultures while crafting their own identities in the region. Dramatically outnumbered by the white population, they resisted slavery not through outright rebellion but through small challenges to the status quo.

And they demanded their labors and their struggles be recognized by the community. No resident of 15 George Street demonstrates this better than Belinda Sutton, a woman who lived under Isaac Sr. and Isaac Jr.'s tyranny. Years after being kidnapped and trafficked away from Africa, Sutton found her freedom. Her enslaver, Isaac Jr., was a loyalist and fled during the American Revolution. Although Royall freed Sutton in his will, she had already struck out on her own when the revolutionary commonwealth of Massachusetts seized the Royall estate.

And yet, Sutton struggled under freedom. She moved to Boston and worked menial jobs to support herself and her disabled daughter Prine. In 1783, she acted. With the help of free black activist Prince

Hall, she filed a petition with the state government demanding payment from the seized Royall estate. Sutton reasoned that her labor had been stolen by the Royalls for five decades and that she was entitled to "one morsel" of the family's "immense wealth," which had been partially "accumulated by her own industry."[1] The legislature agreed, granted Sutton's request, and awarded her an annual pension of fifteen pounds, twelve shillings to be paid out of Royall's estate. She would later file four more petitions asking for further compensation. In short, Sutton demanded—and received—reparations for her years of bondage.

Black Lives, Native Lands, White Worlds tells the story of people like Belinda Sutton. Scholars have given much attention to the subject of New England slavery in recent years, and there have been several public reckonings about the centrality of slavery to early New England life. Nevertheless, the most recent overview of slavery in the region is Lorenzo Johnston Greene's *The Negro in Colonial New England*, published in 1942. Given the recent surge in interest in New England slavery by academics and the public alike, this book is an updated review of the subject. It is meant as a short, readable introduction to New England slavery and is informed by the latest scholarship.

The text is organized around one central theme: connections. New England slavery was actually part of a wider world of slavery and colonization in the Americas, and was important for the emergence of American industrial capitalism. At the same time, however, the book pays close attention to the lives of those enslaved in New England and how their experiences related to larger historical processes.

Although slaves comprised only about 4 percent of New England's population on the eve of the American Revolution, this number does not reveal the importance of slavery to the region. Indeed, when looking at New England's urban areas, such as Boston and Newport, Rhode Island, the percentage of slaves grows dramatically, to 12 and 25 percent, respectively. Likewise, in those towns, slave labor was vital to a number of industries, such as distilling and shipbuilding, and if historians do not account for slaves, the relative economic success and growth of these places in the long eighteenth century (1689–1815) cannot be explained. While not as important across all of rural New England, slaves still provided considerable labor, especially in western Rhode Island's

Narragansett Country and the Connecticut River Valley in Massachusetts and Connecticut.

Demographics aside, slavery built New England's economy and shaped cultural traditions. In the seventeenth century, the region's colonists seized land from indigenous inhabitants to supply burgeoning sugar plantations in the Caribbean with the food, livestock, and timber necessary to function. As economic ties grew, so did social ones. Some of Harvard's earliest graduates hailed from Barbados, while New England patriarchs, such as John Winthrop, sent second sons to start plantations in the Caribbean. Such deep connections helped to foster and develop slavery as an institution in New England, including slave law and labor structures, and shaped the lives of enslaved people, many of whom were Indian captives sold to the West Indies in exchange for African slaves, or Africans who spent significant time in the Caribbean before arriving in New England. Even after the American Revolution severed ties to the British Caribbean and locals abolished slavery within New England, the region's merchants and manufacturers found new markets in other slave societies, such as Spanish Cuba, French Saint-Domingue, Brazil, and, in a patriotic fury, the American South.

Understanding slavery in New England, then, requires recognition of these connections. Certainly, some developments in New England slavery were indigenous to the region, such as the creative yet coercive and cruel mechanisms the Puritans used to steal land from and enslave local Indians, or the emphasis on Christianizing slaves. Nevertheless, New Englanders envisioned themselves as part of a larger world of slavery. It seemed everywhere Englishmen traveled in the early modern period, they encountered slavery, whether among indigenous groups in North America, the Spanish and Portuguese in Latin America, or the empires and states of Africa. Many came to associate slavery with success when establishing colonies and freely appropriated from the examples available to them. New England was no exception, borrowing heavily from other places.

Most importantly, these connections shaped the everyday lives and lived experiences of New England's enslaved population. In short, and as the book title suggests, the worlds created by white colonists on stolen Native land influenced the lives of enslaved people. Enslaved

Africans arrived in New England via the same trade networks that exchanged Indian captives, agricultural products, and manufactured goods for molasses, sugar, coffee, and cacao. Many slaves could remember their former lives in the Caribbean and Africa, bringing those cultural traditions with them. The Atlantic economy that fueled the exchange of slaves also created the coercive conditions under which slaves labored, whether in a Boston shipyard, a Connecticut tobacco farm, or a Newport distillery. Furthermore, it skewed gender ratios, as New Englanders preferred male slaves.

Nevertheless, slaves also participated in this economy not only as coerced producers but as consumers of goods and ideas. Indeed, the peculiarities of the region, such as an emphasis on slave literacy, often combined with larger Atlantic trends to create real opportunities for slaves to assert their agency; defend themselves, their communities, and their families; and forge creative paths to independence. Structures and systems of oppression crafted by whites, however, often stymied and limited slave action. Ultimately, then, the history of slavery in New England was a dialogue defined by assertions of autonomy and humanity tempered by white supremacy and influenced by larger historical forces, namely the Atlantic economy.

To make sense of these themes, this book is organized both chronologically and thematically. Given that the history of slavery in New England was a relatively short-lived phenomenon, only lasting from the 1630s to the early nineteenth century, most of the chapters are organized thematically but still deal with change over time. They examine the origins of slaves and slavery in New England, followed by an exploration of the people trafficked into slavery in the region. The book then illuminates the society that shaped New England slavery, relationships between enslaved and enslaver, and slave law in the region. Delving into the working lives of enslaved people, it examines the many types of labor they performed. The private lives of enslaved people, including their families, communities, and patterns of resisting slavery, then come into focus. Finally, there is a chronological narration of the relationship between the American Revolution and slavery in New England, including abolition. The book concludes by exploring the new struggles created by freedom and the legacies of slavery in New England.

Acknowledgments

This book would not have been possible without the incredible scholarship on slavery in early New England published over the past twenty-five years. The sheer volume of books, journal articles, digital projects, and public history initiatives is astonishing. Luckily for me, the practitioners in the field are also amazingly generous people. The innumerable conversations I've had with them over the past decade have enriched this book. I am sure I am forgetting a few people, but I would like to thank Richard Boles, Gloria Whiting, Lin Fisher, Ed Bell, Jeanne Pickering, Christy Clark-Pujara, Tony Bly, Margaret Newell, Amani Whitfield, Margot Minardi, Nicole Maskiell, Richard Bailey, Christopher Cameron, and Gracelaw Simmons. In addition to being supportive of this project from its inception, Joanne Pope Melish deserves special acknowledgment for helping me craft a much better proposal and vision for this book. I fear I continue to owe her a debt that can never be repaid.

At different times, Craig Gallagher, Owen Stanwood, Lynn Lyerly, Andrea Mosterman, Deborah Hamer, Wim Klooster, Aviva Ben-Ur, Jennifer Spear, Trevor Burnard, Josh Piker, Allison Madar, Richard Johnson, Rob Waters, Karwan Fatah-Black, Alan Rogers, and Hannah Farber have all offered their thoughts and listened to my own about writing this book, its content and scope, and how historians think about synthetic work more generally. Hunter Price also deserves special thanks. He was far too generous in offering me opportunities to discuss (or, more likely, ramble about) the book and helped me work through many interpretative and compositional issues. Chris Friday needs a shout out for his willingness to always lend an ear. The rest of the faculty in Western Washington University's History Department should be acknowledged for being awesome and supportive colleagues. In addition, Steven Garfinkle, Kevin Leonard, and Johann Neem have been excellent leaders of what is—at least in my humble opinion—one of the most dynamic history departments in the country.

As a work of synthetic history, this book did not require many archival visits, but Western Washington University's Wilson Library needs to be thanked for helping me obtain the materials necessary for its completion. I did have the opportunity to work with staff members at the Massachusetts Historical Society, Massachusetts State Archives, American Antiquarian Society, Connecticut Historical Society, Baker Library at the Harvard Business School, Harvard's Houghton Library, Harvard Art Museum, Boston Athenæum, and the Pocumtuck Valley Memorial Association, and would like to thank each of those institutions.

Matt Becker at the University of Massachusetts Press has been a wonderful editor. He has believed in the project from the moment I first discussed it with him and went above and beyond in dedicating time and resources. Likewise, it has been a pleasure to work with all of UMass Press's staff. I am especially excited that this book is published under the Bright Leaf imprint and that it will have the opportunity to reach a wider audience.

Finally, I would be remiss without thanking my supportive family. And Dana, for everything.

BLACK LIVES
NATIVE LANDS
WHITE WORLDS

CHAPTER 1

ORIGINS

IN AUGUST 1645, leading Salem, Massachusetts, resident and attorney Emmanuel Downing wrote to his brother-in-law and former Massachusetts governor John Winthrop about a war with the Narragansett Indians of modern Rhode Island. Concerned about the spiritual wellbeing of the young colony, Downing believed the conflict to be good and just. Waging war on those who "maynteyne the wo[rshi]p of the devill" like the Narragansett would allow God to "deliver" Indian captives "into our hands." These prisoners in turn could be exchanged for African slaves, which would be more useful than "wee conceive."

Downing was shockingly blunt and honest in his letter. He proposed capturing Indians, enslaving them, and trading them for African captives. Having been resident in the colony for a number of years, Downing surveyed the young settlements and realized that Massachusetts suffered from a severe labor shortage. The colony required a "stock of slaves suffitient to doe all our business" because white settlers "desired freedome to plant for them selves" or would demand "verie great wages" to work for somebody else. Land was plentiful and workers scarce in early Massachusetts, and Downing understood this problem. To keep established farms and workshops in operation, Massachusetts needed laborers. And who better than African slaves? As the attorney conceded and Winthrop knew "verie well," the colony could "maynteyne 20 [slaves] cheaper then one English servant."[1]

Downing's letter is important to understanding the origins and nature of slavery in colonial New England. Colonial expansion depended on two interrelated factors: displacement of the indigenous population and labor. Using connections to a larger Atlantic world, white New Englanders could address both problems with one solution, in this case an Indian war. By capturing Indians in "just wars" (wars against non-Christians), colonists could obtain a valuable trade commodity to exchange for African slaves. These Africans would be acquired through the region's extensive trade with the Caribbean, the center of New World slavery. Even better for colonists, as Downing was sure to remind Winthrop, Africans were allegedly hearty and required little for survival, making them a much cheaper labor source than white settlers.

Articulating the racial theories of his time, Downing used his beliefs about African inferiority to make a fiscally sound argument. New England had cultivated connections with a source for slaves, while wars both displaced Indians, opening more land for settlement, and transformed humans into a good to be bought and sold. In short, as Downing's letter demonstrates, slavery was on the table from the earliest years of settlement.

The New England colonies, home to around 1,700 slaves in the late seventeenth century, was not that different from other English settlements in North America. The region contained a small number of African slaves who supplemented the largely white workforce and settler population. Enslaved men and women arrived from all over the Atlantic world, attempted to build lives to the best of their ability, and found themselves exploited at the hands of a vicious, humiliating, and dehumanizing colonial regime.

Slaves and Englishmen

For the Englishmen and -women who settled New England, slavery was something both foreign and familiar. While they would not have encountered many enslaved Africans in England before sojourning across the Atlantic, they would have been aware of various forms of captivity and bondage from around the globe. As such, the first generations of New Englanders had a relatively ambivalent relationship with slavery. On the one hand, slavery was always on the table and a tool of colonization. There was, however, a deep-seated fear about the presence of so many enslaved "strangers" present in their colonial experiment in the North American wilderness. Such attitudes created a legal, albeit ill-defined form of slavery.

By the 1500s, slavery had largely disappeared in England itself. The ancient Celts and subsequent invaders alike, including the Romans, Anglo-Saxons, and Vikings, practiced slavery. Following the Norman Conquest of 1066, however, slavery in England withered away over the High and Late Middle Ages. Perhaps foreshadowing colonists' own predicament in the New World, centuries of plague and famine created labor shortages. Especially following the Black Death (1348–49), which killed roughly one-third of England's population, both artisans and agricultural workers took advantage of the dearth of workers to demand higher wages, rights, and workplace privileges. In the process, many English peasants acquired their own property, becoming free, land-owning farmers called "yeomen." Likewise, craftsmen laid claim to the right to control and bargain with their own labor and skillsets, a legal concept known as "property in labor." Both yeomen and artisans were protective of their rights, independence, and property, promoting a culture and ideology of free labor.

Nevertheless, despite a culture emphasizing the rights of free workers, multiple forms of bound labor existed in England. Although most agricultural workers were free, serfdom still existed in parts of the kingdom. Likewise, young men and women would enter into various states of dependence to learn how to farm, keep house, or a skilled trade. Called "servants in husbandry" for boys and girls in rural areas and "apprentices" for young tradesmen learning a craft, this form of bondage was common and part of a young person's transition to adulthood. Being bound out to a neighbor or local master artisan offered England's youth the opportunity to learn how to be productive and independent laborers.

While this description implies benevolence and a happy dependence between master and servant, coercion and violence were integral parts of this relationship. A key part concerned disciplining young people to move them toward becoming good, contributing community members.

Indeed, by the early 1500s, the nature of servitude began to change. Landowners, both noble and common, began experimenting with their land, turning it over to the production of cash crops, livestock, and marketable foodstuffs. This transition displaced large numbers of free peasants, who became vagrants looking for work. To address this social and economic crisis, during Queen Elizabeth I's reign, English officials, both local and national, promoted a number of relief programs. Many of these programs indented—transformed into servants—poor people, especially the young, to wealthier landowners and tradesmen. The idea behind these programs was not teaching useful skills but rather using legally dependent relationships to maintain order and the status quo. And much like traditional servitude, violence structured these relations. Likewise, to regulate both forms of servitude, English jurists created laws that governed masters and servants.

The Bible, especially important to the radical Protestants who settled New England, also provided an important perspective on slavery. Depending on how one read the Bible, it could provide a powerful critique of slavery, such as the book of Exodus, or condone bondage, such as the various laws governing slavery in Leviticus. Even the New Testament implicitly approved of slavery, instructing "all who are under the yoke of slavery [to] regard their masters as worthy of all honor" (1 Timothy 6:1–2). Especially important to how early modern English readers considered the Bible's message on slavery was how they regarded themselves. For them, they would have been allowed to enslave non-Christians and foreigners or, in their parlance, "strangers." In that sense, the message of liberation contained in Exodus was meant only for God's chosen people.

Ambivalent language aside, many Europeans did look to the Bible for guidance on slavery. When they first encountered sub-Saharan Africans, many used the Bible to better understand the black people they were encountering. They found solace in the story of Noah and his son Ham, who, according to scripture, had looked on his father's naked body after a night of drunken revelry. Upon learning of his son's transgression, the patriarch punished his son, permanently marking him and forcing him and his progeny to serve his brothers. Known as the curse of Ham, Europeans associated African blackness with this biblical story, which provided an important precedent for enslaving Africans.

More concretely, an early account of slave ownership from New England demonstrates how the Bible could be used to justify and govern slavery. Theophilus Eaton, one of the founders of the New Haven Colony (later part of Connecticut) and its first governor, owned at least three slaves, Anthony, John Whan, and Whan's wife, Lucretia. After Eaton's death in 1658, his daughter Hannah Jones became involved in a dispute over the status of Whan and Lucretia. Were they indentured servants, whose service ended after a period of time, or were they bound for life? According to Jones's testimony, the slaves were "servants forever or during his pleasure, according to Leviticus 25:45 and 46." By drawing on biblical law to understand the legal status of John and Lucretia Whan, Jones's action demonstrates how early modern Englishmen and -women used scripture to navigate slavery.[2]

As the various forms of servitude and the Bible suggest, most early modern Englishmen and -women would have been acquainted with slavery. As England underwent its own economic and social transformations during the sixteenth century, large numbers of English people also began to travel the globe. Everywhere they turned, whether in Africa, Asia, or the Americas, they encountered slavery. Travelers and explorers published their findings and encounters with the world. These books and pamphlets found wide readership, as the English Reformation and its emphasis on reading the Bible had created a literate public. As readers navigated the world in print, they prided themselves on being a nation of freemen. They were exceptional: free people in a world of slavery.

As England embraced liberty at home, it could not escape the world of slavery. While travel narratives described the barbarities of bondage, they also demonstrated how, especially for Spain's and Portugal's American colonies, slavery could be useful. Enslaved people, indigenous and African, provided the heavy labor required to extract the silver and sugar that enriched the Iberian Peninsula. At the same moment that English privateers were attacking Spanish shipping and intellectuals were making arguments that New World colonies could aid in the fight against Spain, Englishmen looked to the Spanish to see the utility of slavery in these endeavors. Whether illegally trafficking enslaved Africans to sell to Iberian settlements or purchasing slaves for their own uses, Englishmen, as one historian argues, saw "the utility of slavery at precisely those times when order was deemed necessary."[3] Slavery, then, held the key to making the New World profitable.

Just as Englishmen encountered enslaved Africans in the Americas, they also explored sub-Saharan Africa and came into contact with its inhabitants. While accounts were not in agreement, many English writers ascribed negative characteristics to the African peoples they encountered. Africans were different. They wore different clothing, ate different food, lived in different houses. Combined with the fact that most Africans were not Christians, these contrasts caused the English to interpret them as inferior and savage. While these attitudes were not the scientific racism of the late eighteenth and early nineteenth centuries, these perceptions of human difference helped drive England's adoption of slavery.

Slaves and New Englishmen

By the time English colonists arrived in New England, they believed slavery and colonization went hand in hand. Indeed, even before the English began colonizing the region, famed English explorer John Smith saw the potential for slavery in New England. Deliberately emulating the Spanish, Smith argued that with enough military force, any colonists to the region could subdue the Indians, use them for labor, and supplement those forced laborers with Africans.[4] Given that Smith laid the intellectual foundation for colonizing New England, it should be no surprise that less than two decades after the settlement of Plymouth Colony in 1620, and one decade after the settlement of Massachusetts Bay in 1628, slaves were present in the area. New Englanders were ready and willing adopters of slavery, using enslaved Africans on farms and in workshops across the region and passing laws that governed the institution.

Any assessment of slavery in New England must begin with an understanding of why English colonists settled in the region. Older narratives correctly demonstrate the religious origins of New England. In many ways, the origins of colonization lay in the English Reformation, when England broke away from the Catholic Church. After the split, King Henry VIII created a state church, the Church of England (or Anglican Church), with the monarch as the head. Outside of replacing the pope with the king and allowing priests to marry, however, the structure and nature of the Anglican Church did not radically differ from the Catholic Church. Many Englishmen, both clergy and laity, accordingly believed this English Reformation did not go far enough. Inspired by the teachings of theologian John Calvin, these reformers wanted to return the English church to its apostolic origins, or, in other words, purify the church of its Catholic, hierarchical, and oppressive structures. Appropriately and derisively called Puritans, this religious movement gained traction over the next three generations and was especially popular with the emerging English middle class of merchants and artisans.

Although Puritans always had an uneasy relationship with the monarchy, the death of Elizabeth I in 1603 gave them pause. The ascension of James I, believed to have Catholic sympathies and certainly no friend of the Puritans' anti-hierarchical message, caused many to rethink their place in English society and the wider world. By the early seventeenth century, the Puritans had broken into two distinct sects: Separatists, who wanted to break away from the Church of England, and a more mainstream group who merely wanted to reform the church. James cracked down hardest on the former, forcing them into exile to the Netherlands. This group, seeking to distance themselves from the oppressive monarchy, eventually found passage on the *Mayflower* to settle Plymouth Colony in 1620.

Other Puritan groups likewise began discussing settlement in the New World, especially after the coronation of Charles I, the son of James. Puritans feared Charles, who was a believer in the divine right of kings and married to a Catholic princess. As Charles began to disregard the will of Parliament and levy taxes without consent shortly after taking the throne, he confirmed many of the Puritans' worst fears. His reign helped push colonization to the forefront of the Puritan religious mission. Between 1628 and 1640, nearly thirty thousand English Puritans, many of them as family groups, traveled to New England to help build a Puritan society in the forests of North America. These settlers quickly spread across the region, settling in Massachusetts, Plymouth Colony, Rhode Island, Connecticut, New Hampshire, and Maine (part of Massachusetts) by 1640.

For many of the Puritans, their mission in the New World was an "errand in the wilderness." They sought to create a Godly society in North America combining hard work and piety to build a civilization worthy of emulation across the Christian world. For the settlers, maintaining this "city on a hill" could not have been more important. Thus, order was paramount. Colonists settled in towns organized around established churches, hired ministers, and farming. Men who were full church members governed towns and managed labor to build roads and fences and clear land for agriculture. While relatively open and equitable for members of the Puritan community, New England society was intolerant of outsiders and enforced a strict disciplinary regimen for everybody living in the region.

From this perspective, slavery seems antithetical to the Puritan mission. After all, African and Indian slaves were non-Christians, strangers, and thus no friend to the religious mission in New England. Likewise, popular attitudes held that controlling the labor of others created idleness, sloth, and lethargy. Such sinful corruption of both the body politic and individual spiritual beings, in theory, could not be tolerated.

Nevertheless, Puritan settlers of New England espoused an economic vision that was part and parcel of their larger religious mission. Economics paved the way for slavery. Both Plymouth and Massachusetts received charters not as settlement colonies but as trading companies meant to make a profit exploiting New World resources. Moreover, New England's settlers knew their enterprise had to be solvent. Colonists needed money to build towns and churches, pay ministers and governmental officials, and purchase the equipment necessary for clearing land, building farms, and rearing livestock.

While the majority of settlers in New England were Puritans or Separatists, other Protestants also colonized the region, and denominational diversity influenced economic development and slavery. Anglicans with deep connections to the English crown initially settled what became Maine and New Hampshire. While Massachusetts eventually gained control of Maine, New Hampshire remained a center of Anglican and royal interest. Imperial officials and English travelers, who were largely Anglican, also circulated through the region. Meanwhile, the radical Puritan Roger Williams had a falling out with the more conservative leaders of the Massachusetts Bay Company, leading him to move from Massachusetts and create the colony of Rhode Island and Providence Plantations. Williams advocated for the separation of church and state, and the colony was officially tolerant of all Protestant faiths, becoming a haven for persecuted Baptists and Anabaptists. Finally, many Quakers, a radical English Anabaptist sect, settled in the region, especially Rhode Island, and were often the victims of repression and persecution in Massachusetts.

Religious diversity influenced New England slavery in different ways. Anglicans such as Samuel Maverick and John Josselyn, two men discussed later, often accepted slavery as a natural part of colonization. At the same time, in Rhode Island, the decision to weaken the colonial government to ensure religious freedom created a situation where the colony exercised little power over its colonists. Those settlers took advantage of lax control and pursued their own agendas. It should be no surprise that the colony became a haven for smuggling and piracy, but the colony also invested heavily in slavery. Although all the New England colonies did so, almost the entirety of Rhode Island's economy came to revolve around slavery and the slave trade. Finally, Quakers had an ambivalent relationship to slavery. Many became slave owners and participated in the business of slavery, but over the course of the seventeenth and eighteenth centuries, Quakers gradually turned against slavery and became some of the leading voices against the institution. Indeed, Quakers were some of the first enslavers to manumit their bondsmen and -women and were often advocates for emancipation and banning the slave trade.

Even as religion influenced attitudes toward slavery during the initial decades of settlement, economic development was a concern for all the colonists, regardless of faith. For the Puritan majority, the colonies were meant to be a beacon to the world and send a signal that it was possible to build a functional, Godly commonwealth. One of the best ways to spread the gospel of New England was through trade and commerce, demonstrating how these colonies, through hard work and God's divine grace, could become prosperous. After suffering initial setbacks during the 1630s and early 1640s, eminent Puritans such as Emmanuel Downing and John Winthrop dedicated themselves to transforming New England's economy. Focusing on trade and industry, colonists invested in land to grow food crops for export, built ironworks and brick kilns, and constructed shipbuilding facilities.

New England colonists of all faiths faced a serious economic conundrum, however. The soil was too stony and climate too cold for lucrative cash crops such as sugar, coffee, and tobacco. While food crops—with the glaring exception of wheat—grew well in the region, subsistence agriculture was not enough to sustain the Puritans' economic vision or maintain an equal balance of trade with business partners. Instead, the Puritans exploited the two natural resources the region did have—timber and fish—to create commodities for trade. Most importantly, they transformed wood into ships to catch fish and haul goods, many manufactured in Britain, across the Atlantic. Called the carrying trade, this commerce greatly enriched New Englanders, especially its burgeoning merchant class, and created connections across the Atlantic world.

But an economy built on the extraction of fish, timber, and food crops, light manufacturing, and shipping required labor. As Downing's letter suggests, as early as the 1640s, New Englanders faced severe labor shortages. Three factors contributed to this issue. First, although nearly thirty thousand Puritans traveled to New England, roughly half returned to the mother country, especially during the tumultuous English Civil War (1641–49). Second, given the abundance of land, many of the young male colonists who remained did not want to work for others. Rather, they preferred to purchase land in existing towns or move to the frontier and build their own towns with fresh farmland. Land hunger was a double-edged sword. On the one hand, it meant that New England colonies constantly expanded, fulfilling their Godly mission and fueling agriculture and trade. On the other, it deprived more settled areas of working-age men and women. Finally, the New England colonies held poor prospects for riches compared to other nascent English colonies like Virginia and Barbados. All of these circumstances deprived New England of able-bodied, European colonists and drove wages up for those who did live there.

To address this severe labor shortage, New Englanders turned to a number of strategies. Once again fulfilling their Godly mission, colonists had many children who could be put to work in the fields, ships, timber mills, and households. Over the next few decades, this became the primary strategy for supplying labor. Even as New England's population expanded from twenty thousand white settlers in 1650 to ninety thousand in 1690, natural increase could not satiate the region's demand for labor. For that reason, they turned to New England's indigenous population and Africans from across the Atlantic Ocean.

As John Smith's observations show, from the beginning of settlement, colonists saw Native New Englanders as a potential source of labor. They could be converted to Christianity and put to work on farms across the region. If Indians refused to comply, they faced eradication. Constant English demographic and geographic expansion required the complicity and/or displacement of the region's Indians. Time and again, Indians went to war to defend their land and rights, and settlers captured and enslaved hostile groups. New Englanders trafficked in Indian war captives to work on their farms and in their workshops. Even after prohibiting the outright enslavement of Indians in the late seventeenth century, colonists invented cruel and creative methods of capturing Indian labor such as debt peonage and criminal servitude.

Indian slavery also paved the way for African slavery. Embedded in Downing's letter to Winthrop is the assertion that Narragansett captives could be exchanged for enslaved blacks. Downing wrote in the immediate aftermath of the Pequot War (1636–38). During this conflict, the Pequot of modern-day Connecticut went to war against settlers in New Haven, Rhode Island, Plymouth, and Massachusetts Bay. After crushing the Pequot in a gruesome massacre, colonists sold many of them into slavery. New England war leaders sent captives to the Puritan colony of Providence Island in the western Caribbean, where they in turn exchanged the Indians for Africans slaves. Those Africans, the first explicitly trafficked to New England, arrived in Massachusetts in 1638.

While there were most likely people of African descent in the region before this nefarious swap, the aftermath of the Pequot War created a unique and awful system of exchange of Indian slaves for Africans. Thereafter, in almost every conflict between Europeans and Indians in the region, settlers would capture Indian men, women, and children to trade. The more significant the conflict, the larger the commerce. In the aftermath of the apocalyptically violent King Philip's War (1675–76), colonists sold nearly one thousand Indian captives, some of them Christian converts, into slavery. So numerous and rebellious were these Indians that both Barbados and Jamaica—English West Indian colonies that were among the largest purchasers of Indian slaves— prohibited the further importation of indigenous New Englanders.[5] Nevertheless, Indian captives were a lucrative trade commodity that allowed settlers to acquire African slaves. It was such an effective strategy that many leading Puritans such as Downing advocated war to procure prisoners.

Although local Indians made up the majority of the nonwhite bound labor force until around 1700, African slavery had many advantages. Unlike Natives, black slaves were legally strangers in the fullest sense of the word. They had no claim to the land and were not familiar with the region's geography, making it harder for them to run away. It was easier to control and compel black labor lacking knowledge or ownership of the land. Moreover, while Indians were targets of both captivity and conversion, many Puritans were not particularly concerned with their spiritual wellbeing. Most Europeans perceived Africans as irredeemable heathens unfit for Christian civilization and forced through biblical injunctions such as the curse of Ham to serve. Attitudes toward Christianization changed by the early eighteenth century, but colonists still considered people of African descent, even those born in the colonies, to be outsiders. In the words of leading Puritan magistrate Samuel Sewall, slaves remained "in our Body Politick as a kind of extravasat Blood."[6]

Whether African or Indian, perceived to be part of the community or not, enslaved men and women were in New England to work. By 1700, slaves could be found working in nearly every sector of the New England economy. They provided labor on farms across the region, helping to clear forests, build fences, and plant crops. In that sense, they were both tools of imperialism and victims of it. Likewise, as the port cities of New England established commercial connections across the Atlantic world, and their economies became ever more complex, bondsmen and -women found themselves at work providing supplemental and skilled labor. As the seventeenth century progressed, any observer would have found increasing numbers of slaves working in the shipyards, brick kilns, and artisanal workshops of places like Boston, Salem, New London, Hartford, Newport, and Providence. Meanwhile, as the region's wealth increased through commerce, many leading families purchased enslaved women to work in their kitchens, provide household labor such as sewing and weaving, and help raise children.

That said, there was some discomfort with the wholesale embrace of slave labor. Evidence of this hesitancy comes from the town records of Boston. In November 1661, the selectmen (town leaders) of Boston forced Thomas Deane, a local cooper, to appear before them. Deane employed an enslaved "Negro," whose name was never given, in the manufacture of barrels. Employing his slave in such a way was "contrary to the orders of the Towne." Town leaders ordered Deane to cease and threatened to fine him twenty shillings a day "for [every] day that the said Negro shall continue in such employment."[7] The selectmen's reprimand demonstrates there was at least some hesitancy in employing slave labor, especially in skilled trades. Why such attitudes existed, however, is open to question. Most likely, it concerned protecting skilled labor and not an ideological opposition to slavery as an institution. By the early eighteenth century, such qualms had disappeared altogether.

Much of the conflict regarding the enslaved cooper in Boston probably came from the relatively ambiguous legal status of slavery in New England. To better understand slave law in the region, it is important to look at two early legal documents regarding slavery. The first was part of the 1641 *Body of Liberties*, the Massachusetts Bay Colony's first legal code. Essentially a list of rights, duties, and laws governing freemen in the colony, article 91 deals with slavery. Included in a section regarding the "Liberties of Foreigners and Strangers," it states, "There shall never be any bond slaverie, villeinage, or Captivitie amongst us unless it be lawfull Captives taken in just warres, and such strangers as willingly selle themselves or are sold to us. And these shall have all the liberties and Christian usages which the law of god established in

Israell concerning such persons doeth morally require. This exempts none from servitude who shall be Judged thereto by Authoritie."[8]

At first glance, this law bans slavery in all but certain situations. Yet, when put in the context of the larger *Body of Liberties* and the political and economic realities of early New England, this article legalized preexisting practices of slavery. Included in the section on foreign peoples, the law would not have been applied to Puritan settlers. Moreover, the article concerning "just warres" condoned the capture, enslavement, and sale of Indians. Likewise, the reference to "strangers" sold to the colonists was coded language for African slaves. Within a decade after the settlement of New England, then, chattel slavery was not only legal but also racialized, a status reserved solely for Indians and Africans.

That said, beyond legalizing slavery, article 91 offered little guidance on how Massachusetts would govern slavery. The reference to "liberties and Christian usages" and the "law of God established in Israell" suggest that the Bible, especially the books of the Old Testament, provided the necessary precedents for regulating bondage. Many people in New England did use the Bible to interpret slavery. Yet, the last sentence of the law, referencing those "Judged" to serve by "Authoritie," demonstrates that, ultimately, secular local officials would be in charge of determining who was and was not a slave. Those same authorities would be able to govern slavery in any way they saw fit. Either way, while legalizing slavery, the law left the institution of slavery to be governed on an ad-hoc and uneven basis.

The second document that further complicates early New England's relationship with slavery comes from Rhode Island. In 1652, the colonial assembly there passed the first piece of antislavery legislation in the English colonies. The act complained that it was a "common course" for "English men to buy negers" and hold them as "slaves forever." Looking to prevent such activities, the law ordered masters to free their slaves after ten years of service and were then supposed to free them under the same terms as "English servants." Any slaveholder who did not free her or his slaves after a decade or sold them into permanent slavery elsewhere faced a forty-pound fine.[9]

Rhode Island's history offers some context for understanding why this piece of legislation—openly hostile to slavery in a world where bondage was quickly being normalized—passed. Radical religious dissenters, led by the charismatic Roger Williams, founded the colony in 1636 after fleeing hardline Puritan Massachusetts. In subsequent decades, the colony, built on a foundation of religious toleration and the separation of church and state, became a magnet for dispossessed and marginalized religious groups such as the Baptists and Quakers. The presence of so many persecuted groups, themselves the targets of discrimination, made them understandably apprehensive of slavery. The 1652 law should be understood as an outgrowth of Rhode Island's dissenting tradition.

Ironically, the law also demonstrates the pervasiveness of slavery in New England. Slave owning was common enough in Rhode Island by the early 1650s that an apprehensive legislature felt the need to comment. It is doubtful anyone believed the law was more than a suggestion. For one, when the law passed, representatives from only two of Rhode Island's original four towns were present for the vote. Those towns, Providence and Warwick, were located in the north of the colony, while the two other towns, Portsmouth and Newport, were in the south near the mouth of Narragansett Bay. These latter towns were much more supportive of slavery and, by the late seventeenth century, heavily invested in the transatlantic slave trade. The law may be more reflective of economic competition, ideological differences, and local political squabbles than a principled stand against slavery. In short, as one historian notes, the 1652 law has the "high distinction of being not only the first, but the most widely violated piece of antislavery legislation in America."[10] In early New England, even laws antagonistic to slavery demonstrated the importance of the institution.

Given laws that both permitted and prohibited slavery, the exact legal status of slavery in early New England is hard to determine. A good example of this ambiguity is the legal principle known as *partus sequitur ventrem*. Often referred to as *partus*, this doctrine held that children followed the status of their mother. It was especially important for upholding slavery as it meant the children of enslaved women would also be enslaved, creating a permanent and inheritable servitude regardless of who the father was. The problem for Englishmen in New England and other colonies, however, was that English common law followed the principle *partus sequitur patrem,* or, that children followed the status of the father. In order to change from the traditional English understanding of *partus* to the one most useful to slavery required English colonists to pass legislation changing the law. Colonists in Barbados passed such a statute in 1661 and Virginians followed suit a year later. Unlike these other two English colonies, not one New England colony ever passed a law enforcing *partus.* Nevertheless, it was widely held that the children of enslaved Africans and Indians followed the status of their mothers. Instead of statutory law, as Lorenzo Johnston Greene, the first modern historian of New England slavery, explains, "custom and tradition achieved the same end." Using tradition instead of statute demonstrates New England colonists accepted slavery as customary, rational, and moral by the middle decades of the seventeenth century.[11]

Legal uncertainty can be explained by two factors. First, the enslavement of Indians following the vicious wars of displacement forced New England colonists to create slave law on the spot. For this, they drew from the English common law, especially servant law, and the Bible. Such ad-hoc lawmaking created ambiguity, oversights, and loopholes. Second, as is discussed below, New England colonists drew from their broader connections across the Atlantic world, looking for legal precedent as far away as the Caribbean and Latin America.

After examining the origins of slavery, slave labor, and slave law in seventeenth-century New England, it becomes clear that slavery in the region was equivocal, racialized, and legal. It is easy to focus on the region's exceptionality and eccentricities when it came to slavery, especially during this early period. Nevertheless, a broader perspective demonstrates that New England was not that different from other English colonies in North America at the time. The region was home to a few slaves who worked on farms and in workshops providing supplemental labor. Like New England, there were not that many enslaved men and women in the colonies as a whole, comprising only 7.5 percent of the population in 1690. Likewise, other colonies just as haphazardly governed slavery. Virginia promulgated law after law chipping away at the rights of black people, who occupied an unclear status between servant and slave for the better part of a century, until the colony finally passed a comprehensive slave code in 1705. By 1700, then, New England was not that different from other colonies regarding bondage, as each colonial government attempted to navigate and regulate slavery as an institution. To better define slavery, New England, perhaps even more than other colonies, looked to the English Caribbean.

Caribbean Connections

Embedded in Downing's letter to Winthrop was an implicit recognition of New England's most important connection to Atlantic slavery. Downing advocated selling Narragansett captives for African slaves. Where would he sell Indians to obtain Africans? Winthrop would have understood that Downing meant the Caribbean. There, the center of slavery in the Anglophone world, slaves were readily available for purchase and the need for labor made a great market for selling captives. Winthrop knew the importance of this Caribbean connection more than most. As the former governor of New England's most populous colony, Massachusetts Bay, Winthrop had helped to establish trade connections to the West Indies. He found a ready market for the region's timber, fish, and agricultural surplus, and recommended that New England's merchants ship manufactured goods from England to the Caribbean. Winthrop was even personally invested in the success of the Caribbean and had two sons settle there, one of whom became a successful planter and slave owner.

Thus Winthrop and his family are the embodiment of early New England's connection to the epicenter of New World slavery and source of enslaved laborers. Colonists in both regions deliberately cultivated and fostered this relationship for its mutual benefits. To better understand this connection, we need to explore English settlement in the Caribbean, the rise and importance of slavery there, and how New England fit into this development. Through interactions with the West Indies, New England found a ready market for commodities and captives, purchased slaves, and learned how to institutionalize slavery.

Englishmen first arrived in the Caribbean in the middle decades of the 1500s. Most were privateers commissioned to attack and harass Spanish shipping and forcibly trade with Spanish settlements. There was little interest in permanent settlement, although by the end of the century, a number of ship captains had set up encampments in the harbors of the Lesser Antilles to rest, repair, provision and water, and hide from Spanish retaliation. In the meantime, French and Dutch privateers joined in on attacking the Spanish—and each other. By the early seventeenth century, the Caribbean was a chaotic space of clashing factions looking to plunder riches in the case of the English, French, and Dutch; to protect their previous conquests in the case of the Spanish; or to fend off European incursions in the case of the region's indigenous population. As more and more Europeans poured into the region, many recognized the promise of the lush tropical islands for agriculture, especially the cultivation of valuable cash crops such as tobacco and sugar. This discovery, in turn, fueled further conflict, no longer to plunder but to colonize.

Out of the maelstrom came numerous settlements by the early 1620s, around the same time the Puritans arrived in New England. Many of these were spaces of great conflict, such as the island of St. Christopher (modern-day St. Kitts), which the English and French ultimately divided. Yet, one island avoided the violence and chaos that characterized much of the region's early history: Barbados. Far to the east of the other West Indian islands, Barbados's Carib Indian population abandoned the island and few Europeans had ever visited. Although claimed by the Portuguese, they had done little to colonize the island besides releasing a few pigs that, lacking natural predators, quickly grew to number in the tens of thousands. Despite the lack of interest, the island showed promise. Unlike other Caribbean islands, Barbados was relatively flat and did not have any mountains, meaning most of the island could be put under cultivation. Likewise, given the currents and wind patterns of the Caribbean, which makes it hard to sail east, Barbados was relatively isolated from the violence of the rest of the region. Even better, the large number of feral hogs and rich marine life provided ample food until any potential colonists could build farms. For these reasons, the English took great interest in the island, landing and exploring in 1625 and sending the first colonists in 1627.

Almost immediately, Barbados's economy took off. The island, peaceful and removed from conflict, grew food crops to feed the many passing sailors and soldiers sent to fight in other parts of the region. Settlers salted pork from the wild pigs they hunted and grew cassava and other root vegetables that proved readily saleable. Cattle, and the leather and beef they provided, also proved lucrative. Even the low-quality tobacco early Barbadians grew found a ready market in England and the Netherlands for the production of snuff. The wealth generated by this early plantation economy allowed Barbadian planters to purchase more land and experiment with different crops. Such a dynamic economy also attracted the interest of English investors by the 1640s, especially London merchants. Not only did these investors actually purchase land but they also encouraged exploring the production of sugar, the most lucrative tropical crop of the era. After the fortuitous arrival—for the English, at least—of Dutch and Sephardic Jewish colonists possessing the knowledge of sugar production in the late-1640s, sugar became the staple of the Barbadian economy by 1660. Sometimes called the plantation revolution or the sugar revolution, the change to sugar transformed Barbados into an economic powerhouse and the crown jewel of the English empire.

Yet, this economic development had a sinister side. To effectively cultivate first produce and later sugar, Barbados needed an exploitable labor force. Quickly becoming a "laboratory of labor," as one historian describes the island in its earliest years, Barbados relied on bound labor from the moment of settlement in 1627, when the initial colonists brought indentured servants.[12] As the island's economy took off, it became a magnet for more indentured servants looking for opportunity. Instead of finding opportunity, however, many found sheer misery as their masters, far removed from the restrictions of England, treated their servants horribly and without regard to the law. Nevertheless, more and more servants poured into the colony, especially political exiles from England, Scotland, and Ireland during the English Civil War and Oliver Cromwell's conquest of Ireland. Indeed, by the 1650s, the term "barbadosed" had entered the English language to explain the process of exiling political prisoners and prisoners of war to the island. Treated even worse than regular indentured servants, some of these people survived their terms and were able to escape to England and appeal to Parliament. Appalled by the treatment of white servants, the

English government cracked down on the abuse of servants beginning in the 1650s.

Parliament's action gave Barbadian planters little pause. Servants could never meet all of the island's labor needs, so planters began importing African slaves in the 1630s. Over the next two decades, more and more slaves arrived in Barbados, especially after the adoption of sugar cultivation. Barbadian planters ultimately decided that slavery was better than servitude. Echoing the same justifications in early New England, African slaves, unlike servants, never became free and, as strangers and heathens, could never appeal to king and Parliament for help. They were the perfect workers. As sugar cultivation expanded across the island, so did slavery. By 1660, African slaves constituted the majority of Barbados's population; in 1700, the island was home to fifty thousand slaves. This model of sugar and slaves quickly spread across the rest of the Caribbean, making the region the epicenter of New World slavery by 1700.

New England played an important role in the expansion of this exploitive system of sugar and slavery. The interest in the West Indies, however, actually started with the same religious fervor that drew colonists to New England. Puritans were among the first English settlers in the Caribbean. Most importantly, a group of Puritans closely linked with those in New England settled Providence Island in the western Caribbean off the coast of modern Nicaragua. Although the colony only lasted a decade (1631–41) before being destroyed by the Spanish, it looked more like early Barbados than New England by the time of its destruction. Slaves comprised a sizable percentage of the island's population and focused on growing tobacco and other tropical commodities for export. Early on, Massachusetts and, to a lesser extent, the other New England colonies traded with Providence Island. And it became a place for New Englanders to purchase slaves. Indeed, the first recorded instance of African slaves arriving in the region came from exchanging Indian captives from the Pequot War for Africans living on Providence Island.

Even before the fall of Providence Island, New England merchants expanded their commerce across the West Indies. Much like early Barbados, New Englanders fed the warring factions in the region and,

FIGURE I. An early map of Barbados showing some of the plantations on the island and land set aside for further development. *A Topographicall Description and Admesurement of the YLAND of BARBADOS in the West INDYAES : With the Mrs. Names of the Severall Plantacons,* from Richard Ligon, *A True and Exact History of the Island of Barbadoes* (London: Humphrey Moseley, 1657). Courtesy of the British Library.

unlike their Barbadian counterparts, sold manufactured goods to the islands. It was the rise of sugar agriculture, however, that proved most lucrative for New England. The West Indian islands, especially those in the Lesser Antilles, are small, and many of the islands have mountainous regions where sugar cannot be grown. For sugar to be profitable, then, every arable acre had to be planted with cane. By the 1680s, Barbados would have been one great sea of cane fields broken up by the occasional stand of trees, plantation houses, sugar mills, boiling houses, and slave quarters. Such intensive sugarcane production left little space for growing food crops. New England merchants capitalized on this situation. They sold surplus foodstuffs, salted fish, and livestock to feed the burgeoning slave population; provided timber for construction and fuel; and offered Indian captives to labor on the plantations. In exchange, New England merchants purchased sugar, molasses, and African slaves.

Food, timber, and animals from the region became the lifeblood of the English West Indies. It was New England calories that provided enslaved men and women with the little sustenance they received and New England cattle that powered mills. Indeed, one of the earliest writers on Barbados, Richard Ligon, included a "how-to" section for aspiring sugar planters. Central to building a successful and profitable estate was New England. Ligon admonished his readers that they "must be sure to have a Factor [business agent] . . . at New England." This agent would be able to acquire "Beefe, Porke, Fish, of all sorts, dried and pickled" for feeding slaves and servants.[13]

The economic connections between New England and the Caribbean only grew as the sugar revolution expanded beyond Barbados to the Leeward Islands and Jamaica, captured by the English in 1655. Profiting from the dramatic expansion of sugar agriculture and the immiseration and death of thousands of Africans from overwork, poor living conditions, and disease, New Englanders grew wealthy from Caribbean trade and ever more deeply invested in the use and spread of slavery.

In that context, two important transformations occurred. First, economic relations transformed into social ones. As ties between the two colonial regions grew, many merchants intermarried with their counterparts. Others moved between the regions. Some did both. A good example of these connections is Hugh Hall, a Barbadian merchant and planter. Hall worked closely with New England merchants and had such close relationship that he married Lydia Gibbs, the daughter of prominent Boston merchant Benjamin Gibbs. Hugh and Lydia went on to have a son, also named Hugh, who split his time between Boston and Barbados, attended Harvard University, and became one of the principal slave traders in New England.

The second transformation dealt with slavery in New England proper. Close contact with the West Indies taught the white colonists how to govern and manage slaves. These settlers seemed to take many cues from the Caribbean islands, most likely because they purchased so many of their slaves in the region. To illustrate this trend, let us return to the discussion of *partus*. As mentioned before, no New England colony passed a law stating that children followed the status of their mother. Instead, colonists treated it as a "custom of the country." Colonists most likely learned that custom from Barbados. That island holds the infamous distinction of passing the first comprehensive slave code in the Anglophone world in 1661. It provided guidelines for governing and regulating slavery, dictating punishments for recalcitrant slaves, and outlining the responsibilities masters had for their bondsmen and -women. In addition, the law dictated children followed the status of their mothers, paving the way for permanent, inheritable slavery. The Barbadian Slave Code of 1661 spread like wildfire across the English Atlantic and provided legal precedent for slavery everywhere, influencing later slave codes in Virginia and South Carolina. Given New England's close relationship with Barbados, it should not come as a surprise that many colonists adapted Barbadian statutes as New England custom.

Looking back at the first three decades of settlement in New England, Downing's letter to his brother-in-law John Winthrop seems to be more prophetic than suggestive. By 1700, slavery, which had largely disappeared from England by the early 1500s, was economically, legally, and culturally entrenched. This transformation came about because slavery was both foreign and familiar to the Puritans who settled in the region. While Englishmen and -women would not have had firsthand experience with slavery, they would have understood many other different forms of bound labor, such as servitude, and read accounts of the slave societies of Africa, Asia, and Latin America. Even the Bible condoned slavery. For those reasons, many early New Englanders believed that slavery would be one ingredient for prosperity and success.

Although religion inspired the settlement of New England, colonists believed that to glorify God and do God's errand in the wilderness meant creating economically viable settlements. Prosperity could come through farming, fishing, and trade, yet these enterprises required considerable land and labor. To acquire both, settlers developed an insidious system where they would dispossess local Indians from their land through war and debt, capture them, and then exchange them, usually in the Caribbean, where New Englanders already had deep economic connections, for African slaves. This human trafficking laid the foundation for slavery in New England, but outside of a few statutes legalizing the institution, it was relatively ill-defined, ad-hoc, and ambiguous. Understanding this allows us to better understand the lives of the enslaved men and women who arrived into the region. That is where we turn our attention next.

CHAPTER 2

TRAFFICKED PEOPLES

I N 1718, LEADING Massachusetts jurist Nathaniel Byfield traveled to Bristol, Rhode Island. Byfield did not discuss what brought him to Rhode Island, but he happened to be in Bristol at the same moment a ship from the West Indies docked full of sugar, molasses, and human beings for sale. After inspecting the cargo, Byfield purchased a thirteen-year-old enslaved girl he named Rose. When composing his last will and testament fifteen years later, the judge recounted how he nursed the sickly girl to health, curing not only her physical ailments but her spiritual ones. Byfield proselytized Rose, teaching her how to read the Bible, and she gained "Considerable Knowledge in Religion." As a gift for becoming a good Christian and being a "faithfull servant," Byfield freed the enslaved woman.

Byfield's account of Rose was self-congratulatory. He positioned himself as the Godly person who bought a sickly girl, healed her, and brought her to Christ. Yet, he completely ignored the fact that in purchasing Rose and giving her that name, he trafficked in human beings. He seemed unconcerned with Rose as a person, providing little detail about her past beyond her interactions with him. Byfield reduced Rose to a product of his own religious virtue, erasing her personality, her interactions with others, and her past.

Nevertheless, Rose did have a past. Byfield left a few clues that allow us to extrapolate those details. He purchased her in Bristol from a ship recently arrived from the West Indies. Rose had come on a merchant vessel that purchased her in the Caribbean along with other tropical commodities and brought her back to New England. While ships of the period were notoriously disease ridden, Rose's grave state suggests that she had been at sea for a long period of time. It is possible, then, that she had recently arrived in the West Indies from Africa and after a short layover went straight on to Rhode Island. We also know that after her arrival, Rose married a ropemaker's slave named Wappin and had three children, Dinah, Maria, and Prince. The name of the second daughter, Maria, hints at the possibility that Rose lived in a region of Africa in contact with the Portuguese, such as Upper Guinea, Kongo, or Angola. Nevertheless, given the nature of the records, we can only speculate about Rose's background.[1]

In attempting to better grasp the experiences of enslaved people like Rose, we need to reconstruct the backgrounds of the women and men trafficked to New England, including an examination of the slave trade into New England. Understanding how slaves arrived in New England gives us insight into where slaves came from, their experiences before arriving in the region, and a demographic profile of the enslaved men and women who lived there.

The New England Slave Trade

New Englanders became involved in the slave trade by exchanging Indian captives from their many wars of settlement and conquest for African slaves in the Caribbean. Over the course of the seventeenth and eighteenth centuries this trade continued, but other forms eventually overtook it.

To better understand the evolving New England slave trade, we can look at two documents written during the 1600s. The first is a 1638 diary entry from Governor John Winthrop in which Winthrop noted the arrival of the ship *Desire* from Salem on its return from the Caribbean. The *Desire* had departed New England earlier in the year carrying a cargo of captives from the Pequot War to sell. Having traveled around the West Indies, stopping at Providence Island, the Tortugas, and other places to sell the captives, the ship returned with a diverse cargo of "some cotton and tobacco, and negroes, etc. from thence and salt from Tertugos."[2] Winthrop recorded the first known New England slaving voyage. Yet, the way he wrote is important. For the governor, "negroes" were just one of many commodities the *Desire* brought to New England. They were part of a diverse cargo of tropical goods.

Compare Winthrop's diary entry to a 1680 letter from another Massachusetts governor, Simon Bradstreet. By that date, England's Board of Trade and Plantations, created to monitor colonial trade and set policy, became interested in New England. Notorious for smuggling and supporting piracy, the region had drawn the ire of King Charles II and his ministers. For that reason, the board demanded reports concerning the volume of trade in and out of the New England colonies. It was particularly interested in the slave trade. Contrary to English law, New England merchants chartered voyages to the coast of Africa to purchase slaves. This activity interfered and competed with the business of a monopoly company chartered to handle all of England's slave trade, the Royal African Company. Flagrant disregard of the law and disrespect for the king's monopoly would not be tolerated, and the board demanded an answer. On 18 May 1680, Governor Bradstreet wrote a letter deflecting the bigger issue of interloping but giving us a better idea of the slave trade to New England. According to Bradstreet, in fifty years of settlement, only one slave ship had arrived in Massachusetts. It came from Madagascar in 1678 and brought "betwixt Forty and fifty Negro's most women and Children." Instead of regular slave ships arriving, according to Bradstreet, it was more common "Now and then, two or three Negro's are brought hither from Barbados and other of his Majesties plantations." It was such a small volume of trade that at the time of writing, "there may bee within our Government about one hundred or one hundred and twenty."[3]

Contrasting Bradstreet's letter with Winthrop's diary entry, two issues become clear. In the forty-two years between the documents, New Englanders had become much more active in the formal slave trade, purchasing Africans and shipping them across the Atlantic. Although most of those slaves did not arrive in New England, there was enough slave-trading activity in the region to draw the attention of the Board of Trade. Yet, Bradstreet's letter also demonstrates the persistence of the type of slave trading Winthrop described. Merchants traveling to Barbados and other West Indian islands often purchased a few slaves to complement their cargoes of sugar and molasses. Whereas Winthrop described one voyage, Bradstreet noted multiple ones, making it seem like merchant ships returning with slaves was a relatively common phenomenon by 1680. As the scale of this informal trade increased, it came to characterize much of the slave trade to New England throughout the colonial period.

Even as small-scale slave trading from the Caribbean and other colonies in the Americas expanded, New Englanders became more invested in the transatlantic slave trade. Sometimes called the "triangular trade," merchants from Boston, New London, Newport, or Bristol would charter a voyage to Africa where they would trade manufactured goods for slaves. These slaves would then be taken to the Caribbean and sold in exchange for molasses, sugar, and other tropical produce. Those goods would then be sold locally in New England, transshipped to Europe, or processed. Most importantly, local distillers transformed the millions of gallons of molasses carried home by New England slavers into rum, which was sold across the Atlantic, most importantly in Africa to acquire more slaves.

New England's active participation in the Atlantic slave trade by the early eighteenth century can be attributed to two factors. First, following the Glorious Revolution in England (1688–89), which led to the overthrow of King James II and the arrival of James's daughter Mary and her husband, William of Orange, the numerous monopoly companies chartered and supported by James and his brother and predecessor, Charles, lost favor with the new monarchs. In particular, the Royal African Company, the monopoly company charged with administering the slave trade, had been underperforming and was riddled with corruption. In 1698, William revoked the company's monopoly, opening the trade to any British subject with the capital and willingness to take the risk. New England merchants, experienced overseas traders who had already been interloping in the slave trade, quickly began chartering voyages to Africa. Second, as suggested by the rush across the Atlantic, the slave trade was profitable. By 1730, nearly every major New England port had chartered slaving voyages.

That said, it was Rhode Island, especially the ports of Bristol and Newport, that came to dominate not only the New England slave trade but also that of all of British North America. Most active between 1725 and 1807, Rhode Island slave traders controlled 60–90 percent of American trade in African slaves depending on the year. They dispatched 934 voyages to Africa and delivered 106,544 slaves to the Caribbean, the Carolinas, Georgia, Virginia, and New England. Slaving became central to the colony's economy and transformed it into the largest slaving hub in North America.[4]

Slave trading was not without its issues. It was incredibly expensive and risky. Slaving voyages required enough trade goods to meet African demands and specialized equipment such as shackles and chains to restrain slaves. Given the odiousness of the work, sailors, officers, and captains had to be paid more than the going rate. In addition, risk permeated every facet of the trade. All the standard hazards with sailing, such as shipwrecks and weather, were a factor. African sellers had their own worldview and demands, and were not always open to trade. While overall the slave trade was profitable, individual markets could be finicky or oversaturated easily. Finally, shipping human beings was unlike other cargo. Few Africans were content to be aboard a strange ship tearing them away from their homeland.

Needless to say, resistance was rife aboard slave ships. Rhode Island slaver George Scott learned this fact the hard way. On 1 June 1730, the male slaves on board Scott's ship, the *Little George*, "got off their Irons," rose in rebellion, and killed three crew members. "On so sudden a surprise," Scott fired his pistol to alert the remaining crewmembers, and they holed up in his cabin. They improvised two grenades using glass bottles and gunpowder, and taking one of them, decided to confront the rebels. As they charged to the door, one captive, armed with an ax and attempting to hack through, smacked the grenade out of sailor Thomas Dickson's hand, causing it to ignite another "Cagg of Powder in the Cabin." The explosion discharged all the guns, blew open the cabin door, and injured the remaining crew. Expecting "no less than immediate Death," Scott was surprised to find the explosion rattled the Africans as much as the sailors. It gave the captain the opportunity to open negotiations and buy himself some time. He also discovered the second grenade had not discharged in the explosion and ordered his men to reload their firelocks. They then charged out of the cabin, opening fire and igniting the grenade. Instead of fighting back, the rebels fled to the top deck. In the meantime, they had found guns and effectively trapped Scott and his remaining crew below deck. They fired a few volleys at the slavers, and Scott returned fire, but both sides were at an impasse.

The Africans had control of the ship. Over the next few days, they turned the ship around and sailed back to Africa. Finally, at wits end, Scott and his sailors "bore some Holes thro' the Vessels Bottom." Quickly, the ship filled with three feet of water and forced the Africans into negotiations. They worked out a deal with the captain that they would sail back to the Sierra Leone River and all the adults would leave the ship, but Scott could keep the children. When the ship finally reached land, however, locals came to assess the situation and encouraged all the captives to abandon the ship, which they did. The locals and now-former captives then opened fire on the ship and crew. By this point, the *Little George* was not seaworthy, and Scott and his crew fled across the river on the ship's longboat. Luckily, once they crossed the river, they encountered a British ship from Montserrat. All told, the *Little George* was unsalvageable and the voyage an abject failure. Every slaving voyage was a gamble, and in this case, the *Little George* lost.[5]

The loss of the *Little George* was a blow to the Rhode Island slave trade. Unlike other major British slaving ports such as Bristol, Liverpool, and London, Rhode Island merchants did not have the financial resources and instruments such as insurance to deal with the risk or to cover great expenses. To keep the slave trade going, Rhode Islanders devised a strategy to raise money and mitigate risk. Many vessels sold shares to anyone looking to invest. Large numbers of common people invested in slaving voyages. A cross segment of society, such as tradesmen, grocers, and even women, purchased shares and profited from the trade. Mary Bowen offers a good example of this. In 1793, she purchased a share in a Rhode Island slave ship. Bowen was a not a wealthy woman or the widow of a powerful merchant. Rather, she never married and ran a boardinghouse in Providence. Such widespread investment in the slave trade helped to normalize the practice in Rhode Island.[6]

Investment in the transatlantic slave trade shaped the institution of slavery in New England. This happened in three ways. First, New England slavers often brought their excess enslaved cargo back to the region. Although they sold most of the slaves in the Caribbean or American South, those deemed undesirable, usually children and the infirm, would remain on the ship and be sold in Boston, Newport, Bristol, or any other New England port. Even though they were considered remainders, these enslaved men and women increased the available supply of slaves.

Second, as many New England merchants and ship captains became more involved with the slave trade, they began to acquire slaves for their own households. In early eighteenth-century Boston, for example, ship captains, many involved in the slave and West Indian trades, were some of the largest slave owners in the town. It is not hard to imagine captains, gone on voyages for long periods of time, purchasing enslaved Africans to assist their wives around the house. Others made special orders. Peter Faneuil, the wealthiest man in Boston, if not the American colonies, in the 1730s, was also involved in the Africa trade. His ship, the *Jolly Bachelor,* made a number of voyages to Africa to purchase slaves. On one of those voyages, he ordered the captain of the ship, Peter Buckley, to bring him "for the use of my house" a "strait limbed Negro lad . . . about the age . . . 12 to fiveteen years, & if it to be done one that has had the small pox." Since the boy was to serve in Faneuil's own household, he had to be "of as tractable a disposition" as the captain could find.[7] While it is unclear whether Faneuil received an enslaved boy, these types of requests were common by the early eighteenth century.

Finally, the deep involvement in the slave trade, increased availability of slaves, and special ordering fueled the expansion of slavery in the region. While local slavers provided some of the slaves for purchase, merchants in the Caribbean trade also acquired more and more enslaved men and women for their voyages home. In this sense, the formal slave trade was not so much in competition with the older, informal method of selling slaves as part of a diverse cargo but rather complemented it. It also means that almost every slave who lived in New England, whether born in Africa or the Americas, had spent time in the West Indies. In that sense, Rose, the African woman we met at the beginning of this chapter and who spent time in the Caribbean before arriving in Rhode Island, had a common experience for enslaved New Englanders.

A good source for understanding how involvement in the slave trade influenced the institution of slavery in New England is Hugh Hall, whose father of the same name we met last chapter. Hall's parents were a Barbadian merchant and planter and the daughter of a leading Boston entrepreneur. Hall lived in two worlds, having been born in Barbados but spending a large amount of his childhood in New England. He even attended Harvard. After graduating, Hall went into the family business and became a merchant. Using his connections, he began trading with the West Indies.

Not only did Hall purchase cargos of sugar and molasses but he also became one of the chief slave traders in New England. His account book documents purchasing slaves from the Caribbean and selling them in Massachusetts, Connecticut, and Rhode Island. At the end of 1729, for example, he recorded all the slaves he received from Barbados in that year. He trafficked both men and women. They had many different names, from standard English ones like Peter and Adam, to African names like Quashey and Cubbah, to the humiliating names slave owners often gave to their chattel, such as Dido and Prince. The diversity of names suggests Hall dealt in slaves with three different backgrounds: those who had stopped over in Barbados from Africa for a short period of time; those who stayed for longer in the West Indies; and those who were born in the West Indies. All of these scenarios conform to the standard slave trade to New England. Likewise, Hall noted when he dispatched slaves as special orders, such as when he obtained a certificate to send John Knowles of Hartford, Connecticut, "2 Negros a boy & a Girl."[8] Hall facilitated a unique trade that shaped New England slavery.

Hall was also free to act with little oversight. Colonial governments in New England did little to regulate the slave trade. While all of them had statutes requiring ship captains to pay a small bond or tariff

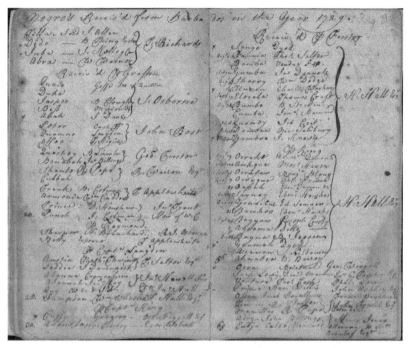

FIGURE 2. Hugh Hall's account of slaves sold from Barbados to Boston. "Negroes Receiv'd from Barbados in the Year 1729," Hugh Hall Account Book, 1728–33. Collection of the Massachusetts Historical Society.

for each slave imported and to receive licenses for exporting slaves, few seemed to have followed the law. Again and again throughout the eighteenth century, Massachusetts reissued the act requiring a four-pound bond be paid for every slave imported into the colony, but it was always ignored. Even the fact Hall bothered to get certificates to sell slaves out of Massachusetts is surprising. It was not until the American Revolution that government officials made any real attempt to regulate and/or ban the slave trade. Rather, New Englanders indiscriminately imported enslaved Africans.

Unregulated in fact, if not on paper, the slave trade into New England reshaped the region's demographics, especially in regard to bound labor. In 1700, there were roughly 1,700 slaves in the region. By 1770, that number stood at 15,342, a 900-percent increase. In that same time period, over 17,000 slaves arrived in the region. The increase in the percentage of the black population was likewise remarkable. In Connecticut, for example, the black population increased on average 55 percent per decade between 1690 and 1770. Blacks went from comprising less than 1 percent of the region's population to more than 4 percent between those same dates.

While in absolute terms, the number of enslaved and free blacks remained small, there were still important demographic shifts. As the number of Africans imported increased, they came to supplant Indian slaves as the preferred nonwhite bound labor force in New England. Indeed, by 1750, there were more African slaves than white indentured servants in some places. Regional growth patterns also cover up local trends. In 1750, for example, 10 percent of Rhode Island's population was black, which should not be surprising given the colony's deep investment in the slave trade, but this figure was also quite a bit larger than the black population in other colonies. Likewise, seaports and urban areas had much larger black populations than the region as a whole. By 1750, 12 percent of Boston's population was black, as was 25 percent of Newport, Rhode Island's.

Trafficked People

Any discussion of slave trading can drown the voices of enslaved men and women, their experiences, and their pasts. To avoid that problem, it is also important to examine the individuals victimized by this inhumane traffic. Exploring the experiences of enslaved individuals gives us insight into who New Englanders kidnapped and trafficked into the region, where they came from, and why they arrived when they did. Unfortunately, documentation related to these individual men and women is sparse—sometimes we do not even know their names—and we have to use context to construct their experiences.

The "Queen"

Of all the writers in early New England, John Josselyn was something of an anomaly. Although he tended to view the New World through rose-tinted glass, believing it to be a paradise with unlimited bounty and possibilities, he was not a Puritan. Rather, he was an Anglican and royalist whose brother Henry was one of the first colonists in Maine. Until Massachusetts absorbed Maine in the 1650s, it was meant to be a feudal colony, owing loyalty to its lord, Sir Fernando Gorges, who in turn provided fealty to his lord, the king of England, in the form of fish and timber. Josselyn made two voyages to visit his brother, the first in 1637 and the second in 1663, surveying both Puritan and feudal New England. In the 1670s, he published two books about his journeys, including *An Account of Two Voyages to New-England* (1674), based off his 1637 travels. Although he wrote more about New England's physical environment than its politics, economy, or society, and Josselyn often accepted his encounters as truth with little skepticism, his account is important for understanding early New England. Most significantly, Josselyn detailed his encounters with African slaves in early Massachusetts, providing some of the earliest reports of those sold to New England.

One of the most important came when Josselyn encountered an enslaved "Queen" while visiting the home of Samuel Maverick on Noddle's Island in Boston Harbor. It was a frightful meeting. According to Josselyn, early one morning at the Maverick homestead, the woman came to his window and "in her own Countrey language . . . sang very loud and shril." Since she had been respectful toward Josselyn, he enquired as to why the woman was distraught and decided he would help her by lobbying her master. The visitor was especially concerned that the African woman had apparently been "a Queen in her own Countrey" and commanded respect in the Maverick household. She even had another of Maverick's slave women serving as her "maid." Such a noble woman needed her grievances addressed.

When Josselyn sat down with Maverick, the details of their engagement shocked Josselyn enough to include them in his travel narrative nearly four decades later. Maverick did not regard the queen as highly as her fellow bondsmen and -women did. Rather, her master "was desirous to have a breed of Negroes" and decided to force one of his enslaved men to rape and impregnate the queen. Taking the concept of *partus* to its logical extreme, Maverick sought to breed the enslaved woman to produce more slaves for his estate. For an African queen, this rape was too much and an affront to her perceived place in society. Josselyn described the woman as taking the act in "high disdain beyond her slavery," and this forced breeding was the "cause of her grief." Josselyn, while shocked, did not dwell on the act, leaving only a half-paragraph description of this entire episode.[9]

What is interesting about Josselyn's account of the brutalized woman is his obsession with her social position. While certainly any woman would be traumatized, angry, and grief-stricken if she had been raped in an attempt to breed, he found the act especially horrifying because it happened to a "queen." In his description, her noble status comes to the fore again and again. Even his mention of the rape being "high disdain beyond her slavery" can be interpreted as offending her exalted position as much as her body. Josselyn seemed bothered not so much by the fact that Maverick was breeding slaves but that the slave being bred was royalty.

Josselyn was very much concerned with the queen's status. Throughout his narrative, he recounted meeting other enslaved Africans but never with the same level of alarm. While visiting Cape Porpoise, Maine, he witnessed a fisherman baiting his hooks with a "drown'd Negro's buttocks." Josselyn did not discuss such a macabre scene in the context of a tragic drowning but rather the high cost of bait for fishing.[10] Unlike the queen, Josselyn had little regard for the fate of the drowned man.

Given his attitudes about class and status, Josselyn's narrative of the queen helps to better understand her background and significance for understanding the early New England slave trade. The woman Josselyn encountered was most likely not a queen at all but rather a noble woman from the kingdom of the Kongo in west central Africa. By the time the woman arrived in Massachusetts during the 1630s, Kongo had long been in contact with Europeans. Portuguese explorers first ventured to the kingdom during the 1480s, establishing trade and diplomatic connections. They also spread Christianity. Unlike other regions of Africa during the period, large swaths of the Kongolese population, including monarchs, converted to Catholicism. They blended it with their own local traditions to create a unique Afro-Catholicism. Through the extensive commercial ties and missionary networks established by the Portuguese, Kongo also adopted other parts of European culture, including language, dress, names, and food.

Kongo was also engulfed in devastating civil wars for the better part of three centuries. Every time a king died, there seemed to be an unending procession of pretenders—brothers, uncles, cousins, and unrelated aristocrats—who viewed the king's chosen successor as illegitimate and looked to seize control of the throne for themselves. And many of these pretenders had armies willing to fight for them. Some of the most devastating of these wars occurred in the 1630s and may have resulted in the capture of Maverick's enslaved queen. King Álvaro IV, the rightful heir to the throne, faced his uncle Daniel da Silva. While Álvaro triumphed, he died two years later, sparking another war among his three brothers over succession. Both conflicts witnessed extensive mobilization of the Kongolese population, especially the nobility. Many of these noblemen took their wives with them to battle, where the women supported their husbands. As with many other parts of Africa, the victorious armies captured their enemies and sold them to Portuguese slave traders. Possibly, the woman Josselyn encountered followed her husband into battle only to be enslaved and sold to the Portuguese.

Yet, the woman did not labor as a slave in a Portuguese colony or Spanish America, where the Portuguese sold many of their Kongolese captives. Rather, she ended up in New England, far from the burgeoning plantations of Brazil or silver mines of Peru. Most likely, she had been placed aboard a Portuguese slave ship, only to be attacked and plundered by an English or Dutch privateer. Privateers were legal pirates given letters of marque (commissions) from their home government to plunder enemy shipping. During the 1630s, the Dutch, supported by their English allies, were at war with Spain. Since 1580, the same king ruled Portugal and Spain. While the Portuguese would rebel in 1640, until that moment, the Spanish used Portugal's extensive Atlantic trading network to supply its own colonies with enslaved Africans. Spain's strength came from its nearly unfettered access to New World gold and silver, but those precious metals needed to be mined and transported across the Atlantic. By attacking Spanish and Portuguese shipping, the Dutch and English hit Spain where it hurt most. Attacking silver ships deprived Spain of specie, while attacking slavers denied them the labor necessary to mine it.

Plundered silver and slaves were also readily saleable commodities. The privateer that attacked the slaver carrying the enslaved "queen" most likely took its living cargo to a Caribbean island to sell. Perhaps they traveled to Providence Island where they encountered a New England vessel exchanging Indian captives for other commodities. The ship captain would have purchased the Kongolese noble woman with little regard for her elevated status. Rather, she would have been shackled and placed in the hold of his ship with the tobacco, cotton, and salt. She would then have been taken to Massachusetts where Samuel Maverick, looking to increase the number of slaves he owned, purchased her.

It is quite possible that the "queen" encountered by Josselyn was Christian, spoke Portuguese, understood the latest in European fashion, and had a Lusophone name. She would have also been thrown into the chaos of the early seventeenth-century Atlantic world. More likely than not, she watched her husband fight against other Kongolese pretenders (or supported a pretender herself), been captured and sold by those same enemies to the Portuguese who benefited from such conflict, only to be plundered by a Dutch or English privateer waging their own dynastic conflicts. Historians have called women like her "Atlantic creoles"—Africans, often enslaved, who nonetheless had extensive contact and cultural exchange with Europeans. Most of the earliest African slaves in the English colonies were Atlantic creoles, many of them from west central Africa like the woman Josselyn described. It is likely that the woman who served her was also Kongolese. In that sense, the earliest slaves sold to New England were victims of the larger processes of war and plunder that characterized slave trading in most of the seventeenth-century English colonies.[11]

The Carolina Indian Men

In July 1717, a curious advertisement appeared in the *Boston News-Letter*. It concerned two runaway "servants" belonging to Samuel Vernon and William Bourden of Newport, Rhode Island. While advertisements for runaways were common in early New England newspapers, this one was unique. The article did not describe African slaves or European indentured servants but rather "two Carolina Indian Men-Servants." Their masters published the ad in a Boston newspaper with wide circulation and ordered whoever apprehended the men to "convey" them to a Mr. Barrat Dyer of Boston. It also provided physical descriptions of the men. One "was a short Fellow" who wore a "dark Gray Coat, trim'd with black, and Jacket with brass Buttons." The other did not require such a description. Instead, the article merely listed him as "branded with W on one Cheek, and B on the other." Most certainly, he belonged to William Bourden.[12]

Why were Indians from Carolina enslaved in early eighteenth-century New England? This phenomenon can be directly linked to English settlement in the Carolinas. Almost immediately after the first colonists arrived there in the early 1670s, they began trading in Native American slaves. Soon the Indian slave trade became a cornerstone of Carolina's economy, providing the colony with an exportable, saleable commodity while also undermining neighboring French and Spanish colonies by attacking their indigenous allies. Over the course of the late seventeenth and early eighteenth centuries, these wars expanded dramatically as English settlers funneled large numbers of firearms to their Indian allies and even joined in raids against Spanish settlements and missions during the War of Spanish Succession (1702–13). These wars were devastating, wiping out whole Native groups, depopulating most of what is modern Georgia, and destroying more than sixty Spanish missions. Although some Indians remained working on the

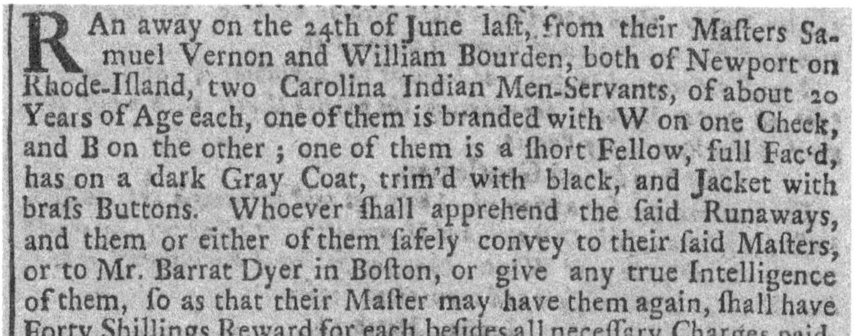

RAn away on the 24th of June laſt, from their Maſters Samuel Vernon and William Bourden, both of Newport on Rhode-Iſland, two Carolina Indian Men-Servants, of about 20 Years of Age each, one of them is branded with W on one Cheek, and B on the other ; one of them is a ſhort Fellow, full Fac'd, has on a dark Gray Coat, trim'd with black, and Jacket with braſs Buttons. Whoever ſhall apprehend the ſaid Runaways, and them or either of them ſafely convey to their ſaid Maſters, or to Mr. Barrat Dyer in Boſton, or give any true Intelligence of them, ſo as that their Maſter may have them again, ſhall have Forty Shillings Reward for each, beſides all neceſſary Charges paid.

FIGURE 3. Advertisement for "two Carolina Indian Men-Servants" from the *Boston News-Letter*, 22 July 1717. Courtesy of the American Antiquarian Society.

burgeoning Carolina rice plantations, slave traders sold many of them out of the colony.

The two Indian men would have been victims of this process. Given the limited description from the advertisement, it is impossible to determine to what nation(s) these men belonged. Since both lived in New England in the early decades of the eighteenth century, they were victims of the "Spanish phase" of the southeast Indian slave trade, when South Carolina and its allies targeted Spanish missions in what is today southern Georgia and northern Florida. Perhaps they were Appalachee, Guale, or Timucua, all groups who lived in the missions and suffered devastating slave raids. Most likely captured by Carolina's indigenous allies, namely the Creek and Yamasee, they would have been marched overland to an English trading post or maybe Charlestown, the capital of the colony. There they would have been exchanged for guns, lead shot, and gunpowder. Since trading in Indian captives was technically illegal in Carolina, the two men would have been recorded in ledgers as "200 deerskins," the going rate for human flesh. Once sold to the English, they would be trafficked around the Atlantic world.

As New England merchants established commercial connections with South Carolina, they began to purchase Indian slaves there in relatively large numbers. Alternatively called "Carolina" or "Spanish" Indians in New England public discourse, depending most likely on slaves' nation and circumstances of their capture, a large number of these enslaved men and women arrived to the region in the early eighteenth century. The leading historian of Indian slavery in early New England identifies a "boomlet" between the years 1707 and 1718 when most of them arrived, coinciding with the War of Spanish Succession and one of the largest Carolina Indian wars, the Tuscarora War (1711–15). The two runaways were probably part of this "cohort." Valued by New Englanders because many had learned useful trades such as masonry in the Spanish missions or on English plantations, Carolina Indians filled niches in the region's labor market.

As the two runaways attest, however, New Englanders also believed these enslaved Indians were prone to running away, troublemaking, and outright rebellion. There are records of Carolina Indians joining forces with African slaves and English servants, stealing ships, sailing home to Carolina, and fleeing to major ports, most likely to look for passage. In New York, "Spanish Indians" joined forces with enslaved Africans in 1712 to ambush and kill white colonists attempting to extinguish a fire they deliberately set for the purpose. While outside of New England, this event gripped the attention of colonists there, and Boston's newspaper carried sensationalized stories of the event.

Alarmed by this resistance and violent behavior, both slave owners and colonial governments sprang into action. The fact that one of the enslaved Carolina Indians in the advertisement had been branded on the face with his master's initials suggests prior challenges to his enslavement. Massachusetts, Rhode Island, and Connecticut all eventually banned the importation of Indians from the Carolina, ordering them to be immediately re-exported. Rhode Island's law is illustrative, arguing that the "divers conspiracies, insurrections, rapes, thefts, and other exercrable crimes" allegedly perpetrated by Carolina Indian slaves justified the law. While Indian slavery persisted throughout the colonial period, these statutes effectively prevented the continued large-scale importation of indigenous captives. Given that colonial officials passed these laws in response to the behavior of Carolina Indian slaves, the actions of the two runaways presented here, at least in a small way, helped to stymie and slow the Indian slave trade into New England.[13]

The Conspirator

Standing on the gallows on the town common in Cambridge, Massachusetts, in September 1755, Mark, a "Negro Man who belonged to the late Captain John Codman, of Charlestown," delivered a speech to the large crowd awaiting his execution. Sentenced to hang and have his dead body put on display for poisoning his master, Mark not only confessed to his crime and offered repentance but also provided a short biography of his life before the murder.

According to his confession, Mark was born into slavery in Barbados "some-time in the Year 1725." He was sold away from the island as a young boy, probably around the age of eight, when he could be put to work, to a succession of masters. One, a brazier (brass worker) named Mr. Salter, was especially kind to Mark, having "learn'd" him to read and "educated [him] as tenderly as one of his own Children." Salter must

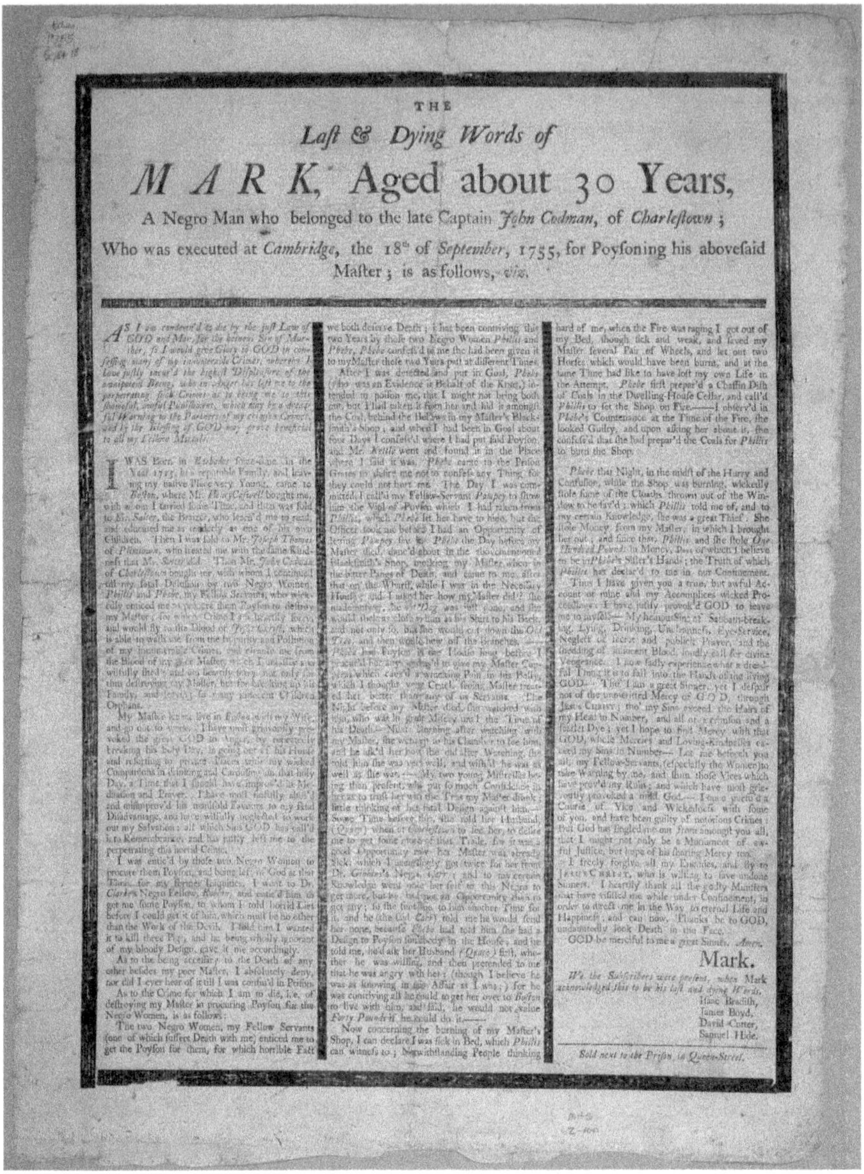

THE

Last & Dying Words of

MARK, Aged about 30 Years,

A Negro Man who belonged to the late Captain *John Codman*, of *Charlestown*;

Who was executed at *Cambridge*, the 18th of *September*, 1755, for Poysoning his abovesaid Master; is as follows, *viz.*

Mark.

Isaac Bradish,
James Boyd,
David Cutter,
Samuel Hide.

Sold next to the Prison, in Queen-Street.

FIGURE 4. Broadside, *The Last and Dying Words of Mark, Aged about 30 Years* (Boston, 1755). Collection of the Massachusetts Historical Society.

not have been that nice as he then sold the enslaved boy to another master, who in turn sold him to Codman. He put Mark to work in the foundry on his property. Mark then toiled as a metal worker in Boston and Charlestown until he finally grew tired of Codman's abuse and murdered him.[14]

Mark's story helps to illustrate an important trend in New England slavery that is easy to overlook when discussing either transshipment or the transatlantic slave trade: many of the slaves who arrived in New England were born in the Americas, namely the West Indies. Called "creoles," it should not be surprising that so many ended up in New England, given the region's close connection to the Caribbean. Potential slave owners would prefer slaves like Mark. Fluent in English, Mark could more easily obey commands or learn a skill. Likewise, Mark would have been familiar with New World slavery, Anglo-American society, and British imperial networks. All of these factors made him a lucrative investment.

Hidden behind this demand, however, was a sad story. The Caribbean slavery Mark knew was horrific. Every year, planters imported more and more slaves into Barbados as deaths, mostly from malnutrition, disease, and overwork in the cane fields, far outpaced births. Mark's birthplace, Barbados, for example, received 85,000 slaves between 1708 and 1735, yet the slave population as a whole only increased by 4,000 during those same years. The average slave in Barbados lived five to seven years after arrival, and men died at a much higher rate than women. Working under such awful conditions, it should not be surprising that reproduction rates among slaves were low. Although birthrates began to improve in the early eighteenth century, arrivals from Africa still dwarfed the number of children born. In that sense, Mark was something of a rarity and thus much more valued than African-born slaves. As a sought-after commodity, Mark's body was for purchase from the time he was a child. A scrupulous master or overseer ripped Mark, a young child, away from his family and community, knowing he would bring a good profit from a New England merchant. Perhaps Mark's sale was punishment for a parent's transgression. Either way, his reference to coming from a "reputable Family" in his gallows speech suggests a desire to defend the character of a family he still longed for after living in Massachusetts for at least two decades.

That said, Mark was also more privileged than most other slaves. The same qualities that made him desirable to buyers in New England would have placed him in a better position on the planation. Planters and overseers often trained creole slaves like Mark in a trade. These enslaved artisans were the skilled labor force on many plantations and often had special rights and respect in the slave community. Likewise, other planters cultivated creole slaves to become drivers, who oversaw workers in the fields. Drivers were important members of the slave community, serving as intermediaries between the whites managing the plantation and the slaves planting and cutting cane.

Understanding Mark's relative value to the plantation regime raises an important question: why sell him and others like him to New England in the first place? As mentioned before, it could have been a punishment for his parents. Mark was also young and not guaranteed to survive to adulthood, a real concern anywhere in this time period but especially high in the disease-ridden West Indies. But to answer that question is to confront the fact that Mark was in many ways caught between two worlds. On the one hand, he was a creole born in a slave society. Even as a child, he would have comprehended how power functioned in Barbados. Enslaved Africans were property that could be bought, sold, brutalized, and worked to death with little consequence for the white minority on the island. On the other hand, he had an African past. Certainly his grandparents, if not his parents, were from Africa, and Mark would have learned about those traditions and customs. Both of these factors made him dangerous. If he had come of age in Barbados, he would have a keen understanding of the structures and institutions that oppressed him, while further being able to communicate and ingratiate himself with the black majority. In short, the master who sold Mark also sold away a potential rebel who threatened their control.

The American Citizen

In 1798, Venture Smith, a sixty-nine-year-old free black man and prosperous Connecticut farmer, sat down with a local schoolteacher to tell his story. Later published as *A Narrative of the Life and Adventures of Venture, a Native of Africa,* this interview provides remarkable insight into the life of early African Americans in New England.

Smith opened his narrative with a short, declarative statement: "I was born at Dunkandarra, in Guinea, about the year 1729." The fact he began his life's story in Africa, not with his arrival in America, demonstrates how Smith viewed himself. Even though kidnapped and shipped away around the age of ten, he nevertheless remembered his birthplace fondly. While an American citizen through tenacity and hard work, he was an African by birth.

Smith provided other details regarding his early life. He could remember the flora and fauna of his homeland and the fact a large river flowed through the country. His father was a prince in his homeland and named his son Broteer. Smith was also the oldest son by his father's first wife, making him the heir to his father's patrimony. Early in Smith's life, his parents had a serious disagreement over his father's marriage to another wife without the permission of Smith's mother, the first and principal wife. She was so upset that she took all of her children and traveled away from Dunkandarra. While on the road, she encountered a farmer and apprenticed Smith to the man. It was there that he learned rudimentary husbandry, a skill he took with him to New England. Only after Smith's mother returned to her father and tensions cooled did his father send for him to return home. Shortly thereafter, raiders attacked Smith's village, captured him, and force-marched him to the coast to be sold.

Unfortunately for us, Smith did not leave enough detail in his memoir to identify his ethnic group or exact location of where he was from in Africa. What he do know is that he lived in the interior of the Gold Coast, modern-day Ghana, and slavers captured and trafficked him out of the region in the late 1730s. While initially named for the gold Europeans purchased in the region, by the first decades of the eighteenth century, slaves had become the area's primary export. Various Akan-speaking groups warred with one another and non-Akans for control over the Gold Coast and access to European slave traders, who offered guns and other manufactured goods in exchange for captives. Others sent war parties deep into the interior to kidnap people for sale on the coast. Europeans even built extensive towns and fortifications in the region. Smith himself ended up in the port of Anomabu, where he was sold to a Rhode Island slaver.

In that sense, Smith's story is fairly similar to other New England slaves. Most Africans who ended up in the region came from two places in Africa: the Gold Coast and Senegambia in the northern part of sub-Saharan Africa. As such, Smith's experiences as a human commodity serve as an important example for understanding African slaves in early New England. He recounted the horrors of the Atlantic slave trade that began long before being placed on a ship. Shortly after returning home from his apprenticeship, refugees started to pour into his village. An army that was marching toward Smith's homeland had attacked them. His father paid ransom to the army, but it sacked his village anyway. Smith's family fled, but the scouting party saw their campfire and attacked. The marauders captured everyone and took special interest in Smith's father, who they believe to be a rich man and hiding money. When his father refused to confess, the raiders tortured his father to death, a "shocking scene" that "to this day" remained "fresh in [Smith's] mind."

After murdering his father, the army decamped and took Smith and the other survivors with them. The leader of the army made Smith a servant to the leader of a scouting party, which broke away from the main group. Separated from his countrymen, Smith witnessed the party procure more captives on their march to the coast. By the time the raiders and slaves were on the outskirts of Anomabu, their reputation had preceded them. Shocked by the conduct of the raiders, the "inhabitants" of the town attacked and captured everyone, soldiers and slaves alike, and sent them to the "castle and kept for market."

Smith sat in the castle waiting to be sold. He did not recount how long he remained there, but one day he was "put on board a canoe . . . and rowed away to a vessel belonging to Rhode-Island, commanded by capt. Collingwood, and the mate Thomas Mumford." The steward of the vessel, Robertson Mumford, purchased Smith for "four gallons of rum, and a piece of calico" and renamed Broteer "Venture," as Mumford purchased Smith with his own "venture," or trade goods. Smith was one of 260 slaves purchased for "that vessel's cargo." The ship soon departed from Africa and first traveled to Barbados. On the way, there was a "great mortality by the small pox"; ultimately, 60 of the original 260 slaves died on the voyage. Of those left alive, the captain was able to sell them all except Smith and three others. The ship then sailed to Rhode Island, where Mumford sent Smith to live with his sister until he could "carry him to his place of residence."

Smith's experience was not that different than others taken directly from Africa to New England during the seventeenth and eighteenth centuries. Even as an old man, he was still traumatized from watching his father be tortured to death, viscerally remembered the horrible ways the marauders procured captives, and recalled the awful conditions of first the slave fort in Anomabu and then the Middle Passage. If Smith, a successful free farmer who valued his independence, still lived with these horrors, it is a good indication that most others did as well. Like so many other enslaved Africans in New England, a Rhode Island slaver purchased and transported him to the region after a short time in Barbados. Since buyers in the plantation colonies often overlooked children, many of the Africans who arrived enslaved in New England were young, just like Smith. All told, Smith's story would have been recognizable to many enslaved New Englanders.[15]

These four case studies help demonstrate the diversity of New England's enslaved population. They came from different parts of Africa and the Americas. Some people of African descent, like Mark, were born in the New World. Others, like the African noblewoman encountered by John Josselyn, had extensive contact with Europeans before arriving in New England. Unlike those familiar with European American society, people like Venture Smith arrived in New England via the more chaotic and violent geopolitics that characterized the greater transatlantic slave trade. Some of the slaves who arrived were not even African. Many indigenous inhabitants of the Americas found themselves trafficked out of their homelands to New England. All were victims of the region's slave trade.

That slave trade had many different manifestations. It began through New England's extensive connections to the Caribbean, where merchants would purchase a few slaves to include in their cargoes of tropical commodities. This ad-hoc slave trade lasted from the earliest days of settlement until the end of the slave trade in the region. A large number of the enslaved men and women who arrived in the region, especially indigenous and creole black slaves, would have arrived via this process. Yet, New Englanders also heavily invested in the African slave trade. They, especially Rhode Islanders, sponsored voyages carrying the region's rum and manufactured goods from around the Atlantic to Africa to procure slaves. They then carried those slaves to the West Indies and American South, often returning with any remainders to New England. Unlike the highly capitalized European slave trade, New Englanders sought capital from across the economic spectrum, deeply investing large swaths of the population in trafficking human cargo.

Both the informal and formal slave trades altered New England's demographics. Nearly twenty thousand enslaved Africans and Indians poured into the region between 1700 and 1775. While the enslaved population never comprised more than 3 percent of the region as a whole, urban centers such as Boston and Newport housed large enslaved populations. Still, rural towns, such as Deerfield, Massachusetts, were sometimes home to dozens of enslaved people by the middle of the eighteenth century. New Englanders even exported their brand of slavery, when eight thousand residents left the region in the 1750s and 1760s to settle in Nova Scotia on land stolen from the Acadians. These migrants took their enslaved women and men with them to help colonize a new frontier. In that sense, New England's involvement in trafficking slaves to the region and elsewhere helped to normalize, rationalize, and justify the enslavement of fellow human beings. As increasing numbers of slaves arrived in New England, the region's inhabitants became more accepting of slavery as a legitimate institution. Condoned and even celebrated in some circles, slavery grew and expanded across the region during the first five decades of the eighteenth century.

CHAPTER 3

SLAVE AND SOCIETY

W̶E̶ ̶H̶A̶V̶E̶ ̶T̶O̶ wonder if Onesimus understood the irony of his given name. In the Bible, Onesimus was a runaway slave who encountered the apostle Paul. Paul took the man in, converted him to Christianity, and sent him back to his master, Philemon, explaining that the slave, now a good Christian, would behave for a benevolent owner. Unlike his biblical namesake, Onesimus never became Christian and was never a dutiful servant. While Onesimus's master, leading Puritan minister and intellectual Cotton Mather, may have envisioned himself as a modern Paul, especially in his desire to convert enslaved Africans across the British Empire, the slave thwarted that dream. Given as a gift to Mather by some leading men of his congregation in 1706, Onesimus resisted conversion over the next two decades. Mather taught Onesimus how to read and possibly write, allowed him to marry and work outside the home to make money, and finally, frustratingly, released Onesimus from his service, though it is unclear if Onesimus was actually free or not. All along, Mather was unable to convince the enslaved man to accept Christ. Even Mather's physical punishments and attempts to shame the slave, especially after the death of Onesimus's two children, could not force him to see, at least from Mather's perspective, the errors of his way. Onesimus's obstinacy transformed Mather from a wanna-be apostle into a failed patriarch.[1]

Onesimus and Mather's relationship serves as a good microcosm for understanding the institution of slavery in New England. Mather, as a preacher, would have keenly understood that he lived in a patriarchal culture resting on ties of dependence. In that sense, his homeland was very much part of a larger Anglophone world and conducive to slavery. Slaveholders and heads of families like Mather would have found solace in this social order, viewing themselves as patriarchs over their extended families, which included slaves like Onesimus. The preacher and others advocated for and passed laws and public policy regulating slavery and fell back on tradition and common law to fill in any gaps they missed. These statutes and customs not only condoned violence to discipline unruly dependents such as Onesimus but also outlined the rights enslaved men and women had. Yet, as Onesimus demonstrates, the authority of masters and the law was not totalizing. Rather, enslaved men and women found ways to challenge and resist their enslavement.

Culture of Control

The world of Mather, Onesimus, and all other New Englanders, free and enslaved, was very different from our own. Its inhabitants believed that people were only equal in the eyes of God, and on earth, men and women were part of, in the words of one historian, "a great chain of existence that ordered the entire universe."[2] This chain created a clear hierarchy where God ruled, monarchs governed, the aristocracy and wealthy administered and waged war, and everyone else labored, their places determined by their skillsets and the types of work they performed.

Even in early New England, which was relatively egalitarian and did not have a titled aristocracy, examples of this perspective abound. Looking at the wealthy merchants of New England in the middle of eighteenth century, Arthur Browne, an Anglican minister who preached in the region's seaports, saw "proof how necessary some difference of rank, some inequality must and ought to grow up in every society."[3] Inequality was not only normal, according to Browne's logic, but natural. It was not something to combat but to accept and even celebrate, as the better sort elevated and distinguished themselves from the lower sort. Hierarchy ensured order and stability in society, as the best—through birth or wealth—governed and guided their social inferiors.

Historians have noted how most contemporaries would have not recognized this hierarchy so much as a "chain" but as patriarchy, the "dominant cultural metaphor" used for understanding inequality during this time period. Patriarchy "extended the familial model . . . beyond the household to encompass all forms of authority." Society was like a large extended family. One writer in the 1750s described the universe as a "large and well regulated Family, in which all officers and servants, and even the domestic animals, are subservient to each in in a proper subordination."[4] English jurist William Blackstone echoed these sentiments, calling the king the "*pater-familias* of the nation" to describe the relationship between the monarchy and the people.[5]

Whether society was a "chain of existence" or an extended family, both imply interconnectedness. It may have been the lot of the lower orders to labor for their social betters, but those elites also pledged to protect the weak. By the seventeenth and eighteenth centuries, this was not so much physical protection but rather recognizing and upholding the rights of the lower orders. These protections included access to the courts and defending workplace prerogatives. In the end, however, it often amounted to little. Elites passed laws protecting their own privilege and, especially when money was at stake, had little regard for workers' rights and incomes. In this way, this social order was less "natural" and more an artificial structure meant to perpetuate oppression and privilege.

And by the seventeenth and eighteenth centuries, this structure faced a massive onslaught that would eventually destroy it, ironically created by the same system that helped to build and sustain slavery in New England. The wealth and opportunities for some European commoners generated by an Atlantic economy underpinned by slavery created a huge challenge to this social order. Newly enriched planters and merchants used their wealth to win the favor of and positions in government, purchase rights and privileges, and further invest wealth in their own vision of the future. Nevertheless, the old social order persisted. Many of the nouveau riche sought to protect their newfound wealth and status and supported the same legal privileges upheld by the traditional elite.

Second, most free people in society upheld and perpetuated traditional forms of dependence. Unlike our modern world, New England before the American Revolution was not a place of universal freedom. Rather, multiple forms of dependence characterized society. Slavery, although an extreme and uniquely violent form of subjugation, existed alongside more traditional forms of bondage such as indentured servitude, apprenticeship, and marriage. Almost everyone living in New England would have been in a state of dependence at some point in their lives, and at no given time was less than 60 percent of the total population legally bound in some way. Children were their parents' dependents, wives their husbands', and slaves, servants, and apprentices their masters'. Indeed, it was almost expected that children would be bound to a master for a number of years as part of their transition to adulthood. Much like the hierarchical social order as a whole, dependency was considered natural and a cornerstone of functional societies.

Concern for the maintenance of this system led to creative yet cruel ways of upholding it. Laws targeting enslaved and free black people were one way, but other examples abound. Pauper apprenticeship, for example, was an institution created throughout the American colonies, but especially prevalent in New England, to deal with poor children. Viewed as not only a burden on taxpayers but also a source of disorder, impoverished kids posed special problems to authorities. In response, towns forcibly removed children from their parents' households and apprenticed them to local tradesmen and merchants until the children reached the age of majority. While a child might learn a useful skill from her or his master, the greater concern was about binding children to responsible community members to prevent instability.

Perhaps the most important way of preserving this system of dependence was violence. Using force against dependents was legal. While common law prevented masters, husbands, and parents from excessive abuse, it condoned a certain degree of violence. Most men and women believed that violence, often referred to as "correcting," was a useful tool for disciplining dependents, especially the young, probably because the adults had themselves been the target of violence during their own youths. Violence could shape behavior and teach people to not only learn and hone skills but also be independent, contributing members of society. Benjamin Franklin, who spent his teenage years apprenticed to his brother, a printer in Boston, recalled his demeaning experience and how his brother-master "had often beaten" him. Violence, however, was an imperfect means of control, as Franklin's own story illustrates. Unwilling to endure his brother's "confinement" any longer, Franklin ran away to Philadelphia to begin his storied life and career. He later argued his experience as an apprentice gave him an "aversion to arbitrary power" that stuck with him through his "whole life."[6]

To better understand slavery in colonial New England, we have to put it in this context of hierarchy, patriarchy, and the violence of dependence. In this world structured by ties of dependency, slavery made sense. Laws and institutions supporting bondage were already in place and able to accommodate another form of oppression. The men and women trafficked to the region would have encountered colonies and peoples inculcated in this culture. New England colonists integrated slaves into their patriarchal families. As legal dependents in New England households, enslaved men and women were subject to the same authority and disciplinary regimen as other bound laborers. Like families, authorities envisioned slaves as part of the social hierarchy, although their blackness confined them to the bottom of the "great chain."

For enslaved men and women, patriarchal slavery was a double-edged sword. On the one hand, they were at the bottom of the social hierarchy, yet the bottom was still a place in society. As such, they had access to many of New England's institutions such as the region's many churches and the legal system. Likewise, they could use the language of dependence to leverage concessions from both masters and society at large.

Nevertheless, there was also a creeping racism that existed from the beginning of settlement. Since at least the sixteenth century, Englishmen and -women had held pejorative notions of Africans. While only occasionally codified into laws that were rarely enforced (with a few exceptions), enslaved Africans and Indians were considered apart from white dependents. In short, despite being part of the hierarchy, they were also different. Unlike white servants, their bondage did not have an expiration date—they were bound forever. Indeed, one glance at the odious laws directed at free blacks, such as a requirement that all free black children be bound out as apprentices, demonstrates that colonial authorities considered being black and being free oxymoronic.

As such, whereas most young white colonists and European immigrants went through a period of dependence as an apprentice or servant, subject to disciplinary violence and harsh restrictions, it was nevertheless temporary. For enslaved people of color, it never ended. Rather, they faced not only a lifetime of brutality but generations of captivity, as the children of enslaved women were subject to the same fate. Only rarely did they obtain freedom, and even then were subject to many of the same restrictions as when they were enslaved. In that sense, people of color, while certainly part of society, endured harsh regulation in perpetuity. Since white New Englanders only experienced that same treatment as young adults or recent arrivals, enslaved men and women, no matter what their age or how long they resided in New England, were forever envisioned as both children and strangers. Slavery, then, shared many features with other forms of bondage but was ultimately the most extreme form of dependence.

One of the few examples of antislavery attitudes that existed in early New England came from jurist and intellectual Samuel Sewall. In 1700, Sewall penned a short tract condemning African slavery entitled *The Selling of Joseph*. For Sewall, his problem with slavery was not bound labor—he advocated importing more "White Servants" to Massachusetts—but rather that people of African descent could not be integrated into New England life. Black slaves, Sewall noted, "can never embody with us, and grow up into orderly Families, to the Peopling of the Land: but still remain in our Body Politick as a kind of extra-vasat Blood."[7] While the jurist wished that the few slaves in New England would be freed, concerns for order and stability drove Sewall's condemnation of slavery far more than concerns about the treatment of enslaved people.

When fellow jurist John Saffin wrote a scathing critique of *The Selling of Joseph*, deconstructing Sewall's argument point by point and making biblical arguments to justify slavery, he successfully challenged Sewall's popular and bigoted antislavery stance. Unlike Sewall, Saffin argued that enslaved people could be successfully integrated into colonial society, since society was already unequal. Rejecting Sewall's racial egalitarianism, Saffin argued, "We are to love, honour and respect all men according to the gift of God that is in them," regardless of race or status, but such attitudes did not mean that all people deserved equal treatment. Indeed, Saffin turned Sewall's arguments about order on their head, noting that if Massachusetts abolished slavery, "those Negroes that are free, if there be not some strict curse taken with them by Authority . . . will be a plague to this Country."[8] Thus, the proper state for people of color in New England was slavery, where they could be productive assets to the colonies. Adding slaves to the population created another dependent class easily maintained by household discipline and the law.

Under Household Government

Reverend James MacSparran was an Anglican minister, a prominent intellectual, and, by New England standards at least, a large slave owner in South County (now Washington County), Rhode Island. In the 1740s, MacSparran kept a diary for thirty-four months. Originally meant to track letters he received and sent and the religious services he performed, the document transformed into an account of the minister's everyday life. Most interestingly, MacSparran made over one hundred references to his seven enslaved men and women. He recorded their work regimen, when they had children, his opinions of them, and when they died. Most importantly, MacSparran's diary places us inside the mind of a New England master and allows us to understand the governance of slavery and how enslavers understood themselves. When MacSparran's enslaved man Stepney drowned tragically in 1745, the minister memorialized the man, calling him "my first, best and most principal servant," and later referred to him as "my dear Servant Stepney." Yet, while MacSparran mourned the death of Stepney, which he did for years after the drowning, even naming the son of another one of his slaves Stepney, he also sold away the child Stepney and violently whipped his enslaved woman Maroca.[9]

How could a master be so paternalistic and benevolent to one slave and so violent and cruel to another? Answering this question involves understanding the nature of master-slave relationships in New England and the types of relationships maintained by people like MacSparran. Masters envisioned themselves not only as slaveholders but also as patriarchs ruling over households of kin and dependents. Almost all enslaved people in New England lived in the same households as their enslavers. Large slave dwellings were rare; instead, most slaves shared space with their masters, masters' kin, and other dependents and bound laborers. Such large multiclass and multiracial households constituted the "family" in early New England. Rather than being defined by the immediacy of blood ties, these families were connected through chains of dependence mostly to the patriarch of the household. At any given moment, for example, Reverend MacSparran's "family" contained nine or ten people, only two of whom were white, MacSparran and his wife, as the couple did not have any children. Upheld by this patriarchal ideology, enslaved people lived in these extended households of kin and dependence, interacting with both their masters and other persons living in the household.

White New Englanders believed the family to be the bedrock of any stable and functional society. Called "little commonwealths" by historians, families were at the center of New England's institutional life and the building blocks of social order. Organized by the patriarch or his widow, these households not only provided a home for the many people living in the family but also instilled discipline. They could be violent and coercive or places of refuge depending on the situation. Furthermore, households were central to economic production. Almost all domestic production—making, washing, and mending clothes; child rearing; dairying; tending the garden; cooking; and cleaning—took place within the home, and it was imperative for the householder to organize this labor. Taking care of such tasks within the home freed the patriarch to pursue his own ends outside the home, whether it be farming, practicing a trade, or more intellectual pursuits such as preaching and politics. Enslaved people were central to both domestic production and assisting the householder outside the home.

It is within this context that we can better understand Reverend MacSparran and his behavior toward his slaves. The minister adored Stepney and lamented his death because the slave was hard-working, competent, and, at least in MacSparran's eyes, obedient. Through his labor, Stepney helped sustain the household and, by extension, freed his master to pursue other avenues of wealth and enlightenment. Maroca, on the other hand, burdened the household. She refused to allow her master control of her sexuality and maintained a relationship with a neighboring enslaved man. Her refusal to comply with MacSparran's restrictions resulted in multiple pregnancies. Not only was Maroca defiant, then, but she also actively undermined the household by producing more mouths to feed and reducing her own capacity to labor during pregnancy, childbirth, and recovery. In return for her obstinacy, MacSparran tortured Maroca physically by whipping her and psychologically by selling away her children. In the end, the economic needs of the household shaped MacSparran's relationship with his enslaved men and women. He treated good workers well and favored them but brutalized those who stepped out of line.

Such attitudes help us better understand the insidiousness of slavery in New England. Historians have often described it as a form of "family slavery," where masters and slaves lived in close contact with one another within these patriarchal households. It is important to remember that this family structure trapped enslaved people in a horrific cycle of surveillance, exploitation, and dependence. They were perpetually and generationally treated as children, subject to the whims of their masters and mistresses, and only valued for the labor they provided the household. Psychological terror and violence sustained household slavery.

The intimacy of slavery in New England shaped master-slave relationships. And much like MacSparran's relationships to his slaves, these fell on a spectrum from relatively benevolent to horrifically violent. Both can be seen in the relationship between John and Susannah Wheatley of Boston and their bondsmen and -women, most famously Phillis, an enslaved seven-year-old girl they purchased in 1761. Having lost a daughter around Phillis's age some years prior, the Wheatleys came to treat Phillis like a daughter, eventually allowing their children

FIGURE 5. New England folk art often depicted the "family slavery" common to the region. Here, a Connecticut woman named Prudence Punderson embroidered a depiction of the scenes of life. Note the enslaved woman in the background. *The First, Second, and Last Scene of Mortality*, embroidered by Prudence Punderson, circa 1776–83; untwisted silk thread, ink on a plain-woven silk ground, gift of Newton C. Brainard, 1962.28.4, the Connecticut Historical Society.

to tutor the young slave girl, teaching her English, Greek, and Latin. By age twelve, she was fluent in all three and writing poetry—and totally exempt from household labor. Interestingly, however, while John and Susannah were instrumental in launching the career of Phillis Wheatley, the first published African American poet, they treated their other bound workers much more harshly. Abner Wade, the Wheatleys' adolescent indentured servant, ran away on multiple occasions, while we know the Wheatleys often chastised Prince, another African slave they owned. On one occasion, Susannah reprimanded Prince for allowing Phillis to sit beside him on the seat of the family chaise. Phillis, more daughter than slave, was to sit in the carriage and be transported while Prince's place was driving—a role often fulfilled by enslaved men in Boston. Even within one household, bound laborers experienced different relationships with their masters that could be relatively positive to completely odious.[10]

Not all master-slave relationships were between male patriarchs and their spouses and enslaved people. One class of slaveholders, widows, were especially common in New England and deserve attention. Given the nature of New England's economy—intensely mercantile and dependent on oceangoing networks—and geopolitical position—in a near constant state of war from 1689 until the end of the American Revolution in 1783—widows, especially in the port cities of Boston, Salem, and Newport, made up a disproportionate percentage of the population. Their husbands had died in shipping accidents or warfare. And many of these widows owned slaves. Given the relative value of women's labor, especially outside the home, many widows became dependent on the income of the slaves they owned to augment their own economic activities and sustain their households. Indeed, male slaves actually earned higher wages than free white females, meaning their labor was especially valuable for widowed slaveholders.

For that reason, widows also seemed to form special relationships with the enslaved people in their households. Mary Minot, a Boston widow, helped her slave woman named Parthenia avoid prosecution. Parthenia was married to Jeffs, an enslaved man belonging to another widow, Elizabeth Allen. Christopher Minot, a merchant whose relation to Mary is unclear, accused the couple and another bondsman named Richard of stealing a chest full of "english coin." When Christopher made the allegations, Mary claimed Parthenia was home in bed ill after "a hard day at work" and that Jeffs came to tend his wife. Mary was up until one or two in the morning and did not believe Parthenia had ever left the house, claiming she "never knew [Parthenia] guilty of any stealing." Mary's testimony was enough to protect Parthenia, and the court only convicted Jeffs of the crime. Had Parthenia been convicted and sent to prison for theft, Mary would have lost her bondswoman's productivity, one of the few ways for Mary to maintain her household and standard of living.[11] For Mary Minot, Parthenia was too valuable to lose and had to be protected at all costs.

While widows and their slaves may have formed unique, mutually beneficial relationships, masters and slaves were not the only people occupying New England households. These could be large multiclass, multiracial, and multigenerational units containing a dozen or more people. Enslaved New Englanders had to navigate these households and all the people who lived within them. Residents in these homes included other enslaved people, both Africans and Indians; bound white laborers, such as apprentices and servants; and the householder's family members, including not only nuclear family members but also parents, step-siblings, and unmarried brothers, sisters, and aunts. To demonstrate the extent of this phenomenon, one statistic is telling. In eighteenth-century Boston, nearly 10 percent of all slave owners also took in pauper apprentices, poor children taken out of their parents' homes and bound to wealthier tradesmen and merchants. Navigating such complicated and complex households was no easy task for enslaved people.

Likewise, living in large, extended, and patriarchal family units often made the master's family members the targets in attempts by enslaved people to resist their masters. One particularly harrowing example comes from York County, Maine. A frontier area, York was a violent space given the near constant state of war between British settlers and French-allied Indians. One product of this violent society was a case involving Toney, an enslaved man belonging to Samuel Johnson. Johnson was an abusive master, often tying Toney down to whip him or having others restrain him for regular beatings. To escape his cruel master, Toney at first imagined suicide, but having received some Christian education, knew "there was no Hope of Mercy with God for self mutherers." Instead, Toney hoped to murder his master or one of the people who helped restrain him during Johnson's whippings.

The enslaved man knew that he would be executed for murder, thus getting "rid of his Servitude." Instead of targeting Johnson or another adult, Toney settled on Johnson's five-year-old daughter, Mary, "immagining she was more fit to Die" and thus making her death "less Sinful" for his afterlife. On a self-appointed morning in June 1756, Toney arose early in the morning, ripped young Mary out of her bed, ran outside, and threw her down the well, killing her. Toney did not stop running, making it to the town of York shortly after the murder, and turned himself into the justice of the peace. Toney was later hanged.[12]

Exposure to others in the household was not always violent, however. Indeed, relationships within the home could be quite amicable, even loving. A horrific accident involving two little bound boys, one an apprentice and the other enslaved, in Salem, Massachusetts, illustrates this point. In August 1735, William Hamilton, the apprentice, and Cuffee, the enslaved boy, were playing with a musket in the yard of their master, John Clark. When Hamilton was handling the rifle, it discharged, killing Cuffee. When the Essex County coroner investigated the death, he called one Sarah Bartlett to testify. Bartlett alleged that Hamilton would have never intentionally shot Cuffee because the boys "loved one another" and had "never been angry words" between the two of them. Likewise, the boys spent long hours together and went "gunning" all the time. Bartlett's testimony worked, and the coroner ruled Cuffee's death an accident.[13] As Bartlett's testimony demonstrates, Cuffee and Hamilton lived together with their master and became good friends, only to have that friendship severed by a terrible tragedy. Such relationships would not have been uncommon in New England households, where bound laborers shared space and grew up together.

While relationships within the household ran a full spectrum from loving to abusive, there is a final type of household relation that must be addressed: sex. Unlike other slave societies in the Americas where miscegenation and sexual violence was relatively open and easy to find in the sources, that is not the case with New England. Rape and sexual relations are difficult to see in the archival record, often surviving as rumor, innuendo, and conspiracy.

One episode offers tantalizing evidence of sexual relationships with enslaved women in New England households. It concerns a leading family in the region. In late November 1745, an enslaved girl who belonged to settler Joseph Hinkley, named Nanny, came before the Bristol County court in Barnstable, Massachusetts. Nanny, pregnant with an unknown man's child, accused two white boys, David Manning, an indentured servant, and Joseph Otis, scion of a merchant family, of possibly fathering the child. Questioning Nanny was none other than John Otis, Joseph Otis's uncle. The elder Otis was a judge and sought to get to the bottom of Nanny's pregnancy.[14]

To that end, James Otis Sr., Joseph's father, sued Joseph Hinkley's son Isaac for defamation. Most importantly, in the course of the proceedings, the court deposed one Desire Parker. Parker had encountered Isaac shortly before John Otis interrogated Nanny. In the course of their conversation, Parker strongly insinuated that Isaac Hinkley was actually the father. She based her reasoning on the fact that "such Instances"—white men raping and impregnating enslaved women—were commonly caused by their "masters Sons." Thus Isaac Hinkley, the master's son in this case, was the prime suspect in Parker's eyes. Even more telling, Parker could not comprehend why Joseph Otis would attempt to have sex with Nanny, when the Otis family had an enslaved domestic of their own that he could rape. In retort to Parker's reasoning, Hinkley snidely told Parker there was a "Difference between a Nasty Dirty whore & a Clean One," implying Nanny was purer—and thus better for sex—than the Otis's domestic.[15]

Although it is easy to read too much into Nanny's case, it does give some insight into the way young white New England men viewed women of African descent enslaved in the region's households. Parker's testimony and Hinkley's banter suggest that sons saw the women enslaved in their homes as sexual property. At least in this case, Hinkley considered Nanny as something of a plaything to be used as the region's young men saw fit, at least until she ended up pregnant. Perhaps Parker was right that Hinkley was to blame for Nanny's pregnancy, but the two men he accused were also, given the possibility of sexual relations between young white men and enslaved black women, liable suspects. The very nature of those relations, which everyone involved in the case—the Otises, the Hinkleys, Desire Parker, David Manning, Nanny, and the anonymous enslaved woman in the Otis household—understood, left the question of paternity in this case open to speculation and defamation.

Governing Slavery

Given that the maintenance of slavery and discipline of slaves was largely left to households, it should not be surprising that the laws governing slavery and slaves in New England were relatively ambiguous. While Massachusetts legalized slavery in 1641 and the other colonies followed suit shortly thereafter, day-to-day governance was largely ad hoc. It consisted of a smattering of town ordinances and colonial acts policing the lives of people of color with little oversight and few mechanisms for enforcement.

Ambiguity existed for three reasons. First, and most insidiously, ambivalent laws and arcane customs actually gave enslavers an incredible degree of power over their bondsmen and -women, allowing owners to govern their human chattel as they saw fit. Second, unlike other colonies like Virginia and South Carolina, the New England colonies did not have comprehensive slave codes that laid out the laws governing the expected behavior of enslaved people, the relationships between masters and slaves, and the punishments for transgressing those codes. Without a unified body of laws governing slavery, slave law remained a jumbled collection of ordinances, decrees, and legislation. Finally, as discussed earlier, given the religious foundations of New England, settlers turned to the Bible for guidance on regulating slavery. Offering conflicting advice, the Bible effectively demonstrated that enslaved men and women were both property and people at the same time. This paradoxical dichotomy shaped how New Englanders approached slavery.

As property, enslaved people were subject to taxation and could be bought and sold. In Massachusetts and New Hampshire, the colonial assemblies classified slaves as chattel, placed in the same category as livestock. Tax rates and who was taxable varied by colony. New Hampshire valued every male slave at twenty pounds and did not tax women, while Massachusetts similarly valued men at twenty pounds but also assessed women at fifteen pounds.[16] Other colonies rated enslaved men and women as polls, similar to the way they taxed able-bodied white men. Moreover, enslaved people were salable commodities and could be used to settle debts. Slaves are ubiquitous in New England probate inventories, the list and valuation of a deceased person's personal property and real estate. Often classified under the category of "Negroes," estate assessors assigned a monetary value to every slave the deceased person owned. Significantly, assessors often listed enslaved people near or after the livestock in inventories, a chilling reminder of how white New Englanders regarded the enslaved women and men living in their households. Slaves could likewise be passed to heirs in wills or sold to cover an estate's debts. Enslavers regularly bought and sold the bondsmen and -women they owned as legal property, and much like probate inventories, slave-for-sale advertisements regularly appeared in New England newspapers. Even after arriving in New England, then, enslaved people never stopped being trafficked.

A legal case from Rhode Island gives us insight into just how much enslaved people were considered property. In 1743, Comfort Taylor, a widow from Little Compton, Rhode Island, accused Cuff, an enslaved ferryman, of attempting to rape her when he transported her across Narragansett Bay. Taylor won her case, and the judge awarded her two hundred pounds in damages. Cuff, although he worked independently, could not afford to pay Taylor. Even more problematic for Taylor, she realized that if Cuff went to prison for his crime or was executed, she would never receive any form of compensation. To address this quandary, she petitioned the legislature and asked them to allow the local sheriff to sell Cuff. The sheriff could sell Cuff, she argued, because the slave was "private property." Rhode Island's assembly allowed her petition and ordered the sheriff to sell Cuff "as other personal estate." Taylor would receive the profits from Cuff's sale as her compensation. Although on trial for attempted rape—a crime which only a person could be accused—Cuff's status as property allowed the court to sell him for the benefit of his accuser.[17]

Cuff's experience with Rhode Island's criminal justice system demonstrates how enslaved people had a legal personhood. After all, if according to tax statutes Cuff was similar to livestock, how could he ever stand trial for rape? Cows, pigs, horses, and sheep could never be accused of such crimes, and the very fact that enslaved men and women faced criminal charges demonstrates that, at least in some ways, slaves were legally people. While this paradox existed in every slave society where slaves faced criminal prosecution, it was especially poignant in New England. Unlike plantation colonies in the American South and Caribbean, the New England colonies did not create special slave courts or bar people of color from testifying in court. Instead, they used the same courts as white colonists and could be called as witnesses, offer testimony, file petitions, and even be plaintiffs against whites.

Legal personhood also came with two additional benefits for enslaved New Englanders, which further differentiated the region from other parts of the Americas. Both most likely stemmed from the biblical influences that classified enslaved people as "servants for life" and thus made them subject to laws governing servitude rather than slavery. First, masters did not have the right to the lives of their slaves, so masters could not kill their slaves. If an enslaver murdered his or her bondsman or -woman, the enslaver faced criminal charges in the same way one did for murdering a free person.

Likewise, enslaved people could buy, sell, and own property. Under traditional English servant law, servants could hold property, which explains why it was common for slaves in New England to be property owners themselves. Enslaved people commonly acquired property from their masters. When Anglican minister Matthias Plant of Newbury, Massachusetts, died in 1753, he left seventeen acres of land to his enslaved woman Lucy, provided she faithfully served Plant's widow until her death.[18] Others made money and held property in their own right. Cesar Lyndon of Newport, Rhode Island, was an enslaved man that belonged to a wealthy merchant, Josiah Lyndon. Josiah essentially treated Cesar as his clerk, teaching him how to read and write, keep accounts, and understand the rudiments of business. Cesar eventually branched out on his own, renting garden plots of land to other slaves and even trading manufactured goods overseas. We know about Cesar Lyndon today because he kept a diary that still exists where he documented his many business ventures.[19]

Nevertheless, while enslaved Africans and Indians had access to the courts and certain rights as persons, this did not mean they faced equal outcomes in the legal system. Slaves tended to fare much worse in a court of law when compared to whites. They faced more severe punishments and could be convicted of crimes that whites would not. A good example of this trend was the crime of *petit treason,* or the murder of a master. A part of traditional English servant law, this crime usually involved white servants killing their masters and being charged with manslaughter, murder, or the like. Rarely was a bound white servant convicted of *petit treason,* which brought harsher, gendered punishments for those found guilty. For men, they were to be hanged and then their body put in a cage and displayed publicly. Women would be burned at the stake. Despite myths surrounding witchcraft in early New England, only two people in the region were burned at the stake. They were both enslaved black women convicted of *petit treason*. One of the women, named Phillis, co-conspired with Mark, who we met last chapter, to murder her master John Codman in 1755. Mark, convicted of the same crime, was hanged and then his body put in chains and strung up in Charlestown. His remains were still on display in April 1775 when Paul Revere, making his famous Midnight Ride, referenced passing "Charlestown Neck, and got nearly opposite where Mark was hung in chains."[20] As the horrific punishments meted out to Mark and Phillis suggest, having access to the courts did not mean equal treatment. Indeed, given the ad hoc nature of governing slavery, the court system was one of the chief vehicles for racializing African and Indian slaves, ensuring that they received different treatment based on the color of their skin.

Eventually the colonies codified some of these different punishments into law. As the case of Cuff above demonstrates, rarely could enslaved people pay fines and restitution if they had been found guilty of crimes. Instead, the colonies substituted corporal punishment, up to thirty lashes in the case of Connecticut, for this inability to pay. Whites would only receive such punishments if they were indigent or found in collusion with people of color. Likewise, enslaved men and women, unlike even bound whites, faced the possibility of banishment, being sold to the southern colonies or West Indies, as punishment.

Beyond this unequal treatment, New England towns and colonial legislatures did pass different laws governing slave behavior. Like disproportionate judicial punishments, these acts had the effect of racializing the region's population, as many of these regulations directly targeted "Indians, mulattos, and Negroes," thus making them subject to restrictions the white population did not face and placing them under constant surveillance. This created a situation where the courts punished people of color, towns and colonies created codes that criminalized their behavior, and entire communities watched them for any wrong doing.

Numerous examples of these codes and statutes exist. First, every New England colony passed curfews, usually nine o'clock in the evening, on Indian and African slaves and free blacks. These curfews were meant to prevent supposed criminal behavior. Massachusetts passed one to prevent the "disorders, insolencies, and burglaries" allegedly perpetrated by people of color at night, while Connecticut included their curfew as part of a law preventing running away in 1703. Many towns and some of the colonies also had laws preventing the sale of alcohol, believing that it made bound workers harder to control. Likewise, all the New England colonies passed laws preventing people of color from attacking or defaming whites. In Connecticut, transgressors of this law could be whipped up to forty times. Finally, towns and colonies approved rules preventing the congregation of large numbers of people of color and whites' harboring groups of slaves. By 1750, Rhode Island fined whites up to fifty pounds or imprisoned them for a month if they hosted enslaved people without the permission of their masters. As such, these statutes not only racialized people of color but also sought to separate them from whites as much as possible.

Two of these codes deserve special attention. First were laws against miscegenation and the intermarriage of whites and blacks. Unlike the southern and Caribbean colonies, where these laws were ubiquitous by the middle decades of the seventeenth century, only one New England colony, Massachusetts, passed a law preventing miscegenation. And it was much later, coming in 1705. Called "An Act for the Better Preventing of a Spurious and Mixt Issue," the law prohibited intermarriage and fornication between blacks and whites. There were heavy penalties, including whippings and fines up to fifty pounds, for anyone found in violation of the act or illegally facilitating intermarriage or fornication. While it did not prevent interracial fornication, perhaps the act did have a silencing effect on sexual acts, which explains why sex within the household is hard to find in the records. Colonists in other parts of New England did not pass similar acts but would have nevertheless agreed with the ultimate purpose of the Massachusetts law: preventing interracial marriage and sex and marginalizing, separating, and differentiating people of color.

Second, as the law against intermarriage suggests, some of the legislation aimed at controlling slaves was also meant to control the behavior of masters. Manumission, or the act of freeing enslaved people, is a good example. Heavily regulated by the state, manumission was meant to reward the faithful and trusty service of loyal bondsmen and -women. Instead, many enslavers would free old and indigent slaves so they would no longer have to care for the formerly enslaved. In response, every New England colony passed laws to prevent this practice. Fearing that freed slaves would be a burden on the community, Massachusetts and Rhode Island required masters to post a bond, fifty pounds in the case of Massachusetts, to provide for the freed person if that person could not support him- or herself. Connecticut empowered towns to seek compensation from former masters and their heirs if any manumitted person took public monies. These laws were fairly effective at preventing manumissions and help to explain the relatively small free black population in colonial New England.

Despite the low manumission rate, racialization, and segregation, it is important to note that the attempts by colonies and towns to govern slavery often granted privileges or went totally unenforced. In the 1705 act preventing interracial marriage in Massachusetts, for example, the law legalized marriage between enslaved men and women. This provision, included at the behest of Samuel Sewall, backed slave marriages with the force of law, making it difficult for owners to break enslaved spouses apart. Moreover, some of these acts conformed with older Puritan laws, prohibiting enslaved people from working on Sundays, thus giving them a day for rest, relaxation, and recreation. Finally, many of these codes went unenforced and ignored. Boston passed a curfew multiple times during the eighteenth century but rarely were enslaved people punished for violating it. An exasperated letter to the *Boston News Letter* from 1738 suggests the frustration of some over the lack of enforcement. In it, the author expressed dismay and even went so far as to have the curfew act reprinted in full, arguing that the enforcement of the act would "promote good Orders" and imploring "all Masters or Owners of any Indian, Negro or Molatto Servants" to "take effectual Care" that their "Servants" would be inside by "Nine a Clock."[21] Despite this plea, the curfew continued to go largely unenforced.

Enslaved New Englanders lived in a world characterized by hierarchy, dependence, and bondage. Such a socially stratified world had important effects on the lives of slaves and the way the institution of slavery functioned. Enslaved people were very much part of that hierarchy, but their race and subservient status confined them to the bottom of the social order. Often living and working in households under the guise of a patriarch, bondsmen and -women confronted this system in its most intimate form. For that reason, relations between masters and slaves and between enslaved people and other dependents in the household varied widely. Some were amicable, while others were horrific, as enslaved people faced intimate and sexual violence.

Although much of the governance of slavery was left to these patriarchal households, colonies and towns did attempt to regulate slavery. Being defined as both people and property forced slaves to navigate and be subject to a paradoxical status. While the legal systems of these colonies tended to be relatively open, especially when compared to those in plantation colonies, enslaved men and women were by no means equal under the law. Between the courts and specific acts targeting people of color, towns and colonies effectively racialized the population and made race an important component of the social order. Racialization may have been the end product of these laws, but their original intention was to maintain a bound, marginalized, and compliant labor force. Despite the hopes of colonial policymakers, the working lives of enslaved New Englanders were far too dynamic to be controlled by ambiguous legislation.

CHAPTER 4

WORKING WORLDS

W HEN LOOKING FOR the presence of enslaved people in early New England, we do not have to look much further than newspapers. There, African and Indian slaves appeared in stories, accounts of runaways, and, perhaps most commonly, for-sale and for-hire advertisements. These last often described enslaved men and women as "fit for town or country" work, suggesting just how flexible and dynamic slave labor was in early New England. Indeed, colonists spent a considerable amount of time acquiring and training slaves to meet New England's many labor demands. In doing so, they created a flexible, skilled, and, most importantly, effective workforce.

It is important to explore the labor performed by enslaved men and women in the region. They comprised a vibrant, skilled workforce that formed an important component of the region's economic life and could be found laboring in every sector of New England's economy, although they were particularly important for household work; industrial enterprises, such as shipbuilding and distilling; and both large-scale and subsistence agriculture. We cannot, however, blindly label work as drudgery foisted on slaves by enslavers. Labor brought useful skills, built associations and solidarity with fellow free and unfree workers, and offered material benefits. For enslaved men and women in New England, work had meaning beyond toil.

Work Culture

When English settlers arrived in New England during the 1620s and 1630s, they established certain patterns of working that shaped slave labor in the region. New Englanders' lives revolved around the household, which, in addition to being the basic unit of social organization, was also the basic unit of economic organization. Household heads commanded the labor of all those living under their purview. For most New Englanders, profits from farming stony soil or working in developing urban economies were meager. With such small earnings, it was hard to purchase bound labor—enslaved or indentured—and most families relied on the work of their own children, which also accounts for why white New Englanders had so many kids. Small profits and large families further help explain why slaveholding remained relatively limited, usually with families owning no more than one or two slaves, in New England.

Despite these broad trends, there was a general divide between agricultural labor, often performed in rural areas, and industrial production, often performed by skilled artisans in towns. Nevertheless, even Boston, New England's largest town, still had orchards and cattle roaming the streets in the eighteenth century. That said, most heavy industrial production, such as shipbuilding and distilling, took place in the large port towns, such as Boston, Newport, Plymouth, Salem, and New London, while major agricultural production took place in rural areas, especially those with fertile soil such as the Connecticut River Valley and Narragansett Country in Rhode Island and Connecticut.

Moreover, labor was highly gendered in early New England. Although there are examples of many women becoming entrepreneurs, women's work was, in theory at least, confined to the household. They made and mended clothes, raised the children, tended the garden, prepared food, milked the cows, and kept house. These tasks fell under the purview of "household production" and were instrumental in providing men with the time to pursue work outside the home. In farming communities, men would be the ones to till the fields and maintain the crops, while in urban areas, they would work in workshops or multiple endeavors. Enslaved people largely followed these patterns of gendered work, which means that while enslaved women's work did not vary widely between urban and rural areas, men's work would have been dramatically different depending on location.

Slavery conformed to other larger trends in New England's labor market, including the practice of lending or hiring enslaved workers out to fellow colonists. Many New England families swapped their children with other families or hired them out to others in need of labor. It was common, for example, for farm boys living in Essex County, Massachusetts, to join fishing expeditions during their teenage years to make their own wages. Enslaved people could expect the same treatment. The conditions of hiring out varied, but New England's newspapers are full of examples. One 1754 advertisement offered four slaves— three men and one woman—for hire. The men were highly skilled, with one being a tailor, one fit "either for Town or Country" work, and the fourth a skilled violinist.[1] While they would not have been hired out together, it is easy to envision a wealthy long-term visitor seeing an opportunity in this advertisement. The visitor could hire someone to repair clothes, do work around the property, and entertain guests with a violin, a specialty of West African musicians, while the enslaved woman was available to perform domestic duties. For masters, hiring out slaves meant that the owners were able to minimize idleness and ensure their enslaved property constantly generated revenue.

Other slave owners allowed their slaves to effectively be journeymen and -women, traveling New England's towns and farms, hiring themselves out, negotiating their own wages and working conditions, and remitting some of those back to their masters. Mark, the enslaved man from Barbados who resided with his master, John Codman, in Charlestown, Massachusetts, received permission from Codman to live and work in Boston. Far from his master's purview, Mark established a forge where he did metalwork for locals. He also made enough money to rent a place to live and establish a family with a local black woman. Like hiring their slaves out, masters ensured their slaves remained employed and productive by allowing them to negotiate their own employment situations. Of course, this also meant slaveholders abdicated their responsibility for feeding or housing their slaves, ultimately saving the owners money.

To be Sold by BENJAMIN CHURCH *at his usual Place of Sale, on Thursday next.*

A Percel of Stotch Linnens yard wide & 7 8lbs, and Houshold Furniture of sundry Sorts, wearing Apparel, and a large Silver Bowl, &c.&c.

TO be Sold on Friday next the 25th Instant, at One o'Clock, at the Houfe of Capt. *Robert Stone* in King-ftreet ; a new Englifh Cable, 10 Inches thick, and 100 Fathom long ; with a Quantity of Sheathing Nails. Any Perfon who has a Mind to purchafe the Cable, may fee it any Time before the Sale at Major *Noble's* Warehoufe on *Hearfey's* Wharffe.

TO be hired out a young Negro Man Taylor, who works well at the Trade ; a young Negro Man fit either for Town or Country ; a Negro Man that plays well on the Violin and a Negro Girl fit to attend a Family. Inquire of the Printer

TO be Sold by *Nathanael Ralfton*, Efq; of *Bofton*,

FIGURE 6. An eighteenth-century hiring-out ad from the *Boston Gazette,* 22 January 1754. Collection of the Massachusetts Historical Society.

Venture Smith, the freedman who we met in chapter 2, offers insight into how the process of self-hire functioned. In his narrative, Smith described the negotiations he had with his master, a Colonel O. Smith. Smith, whose last name Venture ultimately took, was his third master since arriving in Connecticut. He had a rough-and-tumble relationship with his former owners, including coming to fisticuffs with one, but was generally a hard worker. Colonel Smith valued that work ethic and purchased Venture. The enslaved man saw this as an opportunity and was able to negotiate with the colonel to work on his own during the winter months. His master agreed under the condition Smith would "give him one quarter of my earnings."

This ability to find his own employment, however, was not guaranteed. The following spring, Venture approached Colonel Smith about "going out to work" on his own again. This time, the colonel refused. He informed Venture that "he must have [Venture's] labor this summer," given the needs of his farm. Venture, never one to take no for an answer, pleaded with the colonel. He told his master that he considered it unfair that "I could not have a chance to work out when the season became advantageous" and that he was only "permitted to hire [himself] out" during winter, "the poorest season of the year." Colonel Smith saw an opportunity and asked Venture what he "would give him for the privilege" of hiring out. The slave replied, two pounds per month. That was a sizable sum of money, and the colonel agreed to these terms.[2]

In the negotiation between Smith and his master, we can see that self-hiring was often a negotiation and often only permitted when the master did not require the slave's labor. Indeed, self-hire was another strategy to avoid idleness. Likewise, these negotiations also demonstrate how lucrative self-hiring could be for the master. During the winter time, Colonel Smith received a quarter of Venture's earnings, while summer self-employment brought Smith two pounds a month. Wages in colonial New England were higher than other places, but two pounds a month was the equivalent of what a tradesman would make. For Colonel Smith, then, having Venture remit that amount of cash every month was like having an additional laborer working in his household while not having to provide for his food and lodging.

Understanding hiring and self-hiring also forces us to confront who owned slaves in New England. By the 1720s, the majority of slave owners in New England towns were not wealthy merchants but rather craftsmen and farmers, suggesting that even with a general reliance on familial labor, slavery was a key component of New England's labor system. Given that artisans and yeomen comprised the equivalent of what we would today call the "middle class"—colonists used the term "middling"—it is important to understand both why people would own slaves and what this meant for society as a whole.

For that, we can look to other eighteenth-century slave societies. One historian of Jamaica has identified three reasons why people owned slaves during this period. First, and most obviously, slaves provided labor at low cost. Wages for free workers, even unskilled ones, were high in early New England, cutting into profits. Enslaved labor, on the other hand, was relatively affordable. After an initial purchase cost, which could be worked off in a few short years, all masters had to do was provide adequate food and shelter for their slaves to continue working. Even better, many masters allowed slaves to work for themselves under the condition they provided for their own subsistence. Second, enslaved people were an investment that appreciated over time. This phenomenon was especially true in New England, where artisans purchased boys and girls on the cheap and trained them in a skill as they grew to adulthood. By the time their master had retired or died, the enslaved person had become quite valuable. Third, and related to the second, enslaved people were readily salable. If a master died in debt, enslaved people could always be sold. While living, if the master became short on cash, an enslaved person could be sold.[3]

These three rationales for owning slaves also speak to the effect that middling slave owning had on New England. Slaveholding was not exclusively the purview of the wealthy but rather was spread throughout society. Thus, a very large segment of New England's population became beholden to slavery. And it went beyond actual slave ownership. Even New Englanders who did not own slaves benefited from its presence. Enslaved people were consumers, meaning like other colonists, they required things like shoes, food, and clothing. Cordwainers (shoemakers), vendors, and tailors were more than happy to oblige. Even professionals, such as medical doctors and ministers, benefited as slaves became patients and parishioners. Thus, widespread slave ownership meant even more widespread investment in slavery as an institution. Only a cataclysmic political event—the American Revolution—would bring about its demise.

The commitment to slave labor demonstrates how valuable it was to New England, and that value created opportunities for enslaved people. At its base level, slavery provided some, though not guaranteed, protection. Masters would think twice about violently abusing or selling a piece of property that was so valuable to their estate. Yet, even more tangibly, that value created opportunities for being hired out, self-hiring, and earning wages. These in turn allowed enslaved men and women to find autonomy from their masters and mistresses and participate in a growing consumer economy. Earning wages and managing one's own time also created more significant opportunities. Venture Smith again provides a good example. Smith, both because of his own obstinacy and the labor needs of rural Connecticut, had three different masters by the time he was in his early thirties. His last master, Colonel Smith, offered Venture a once-in-a-lifetime opportunity: to purchase his own freedom. Venture, already hiring himself out and working on his own time, leaped at the possibility, and within five years was a free man. As the life of Venture Smith and many other enslaved people demonstrates, work had meaning. It was not only a form of drudgery foisted on enslaved New Englanders but an act that created opportunities and possibilities.

Urban Spaces

In terms of sheer numbers, most enslaved New Englanders lived in the region's major towns and seaports. By 1750, Boston alone was home to more than 1,500 slaves or roughly 10 percent of the total number of enslaved people in New England. Seaports were disproportionately black. Whereas some rural towns only had one or two slaves in the middle decades of the eighteenth century, Newport, Rhode Island's enslaved population comprised 25 percent of the total. While slavery was both an urban and rural phenomenon in New England, these population figures demonstrate just how vital enslaved laborers were to town and port economies. Slaves worked in every conceivable trade and workplace, serving in households, workshops, industrial sites, and many maritime occupations. Indeed, the last two places of employment— industry and the sea—reinforced one another as the acquisition of slave labor allowed craftsmen to expand industrial production, which in turn led to an increase in overseas trade and the need for more maritime labor. Like tradespeople, merchants and ship captains turned to slaves to fill this need. Moreover, these labor needs shaped the demography of urban slavery in New England as a majority were men, although women could be found in households and marketplaces.

By the 1740s, nearly one in four households in Boston and one in three households in Newport owned slaves. Many of these people remained in their masters' households providing domestic labor. Those who used slaves as household labor tended to be wealthier, although poorer slave-holders and widows would often hire out domestic labor to wealthier families and visitors. Much like the economy as a whole, there was a divide between the domestic labor performed by men and women.

Enslaved women working in New England's urban households were key figures in the region's domestic economy. They cooked meals,

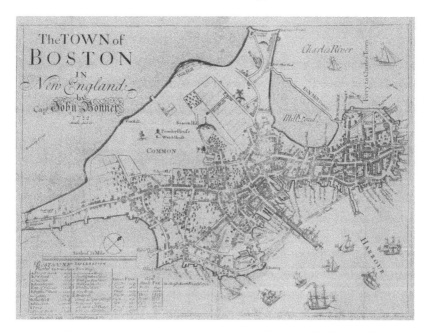

FIGURE 7. Boston in the eighteenth century. John Bonner, *The Town of Boston in New England* (Boston: Francis Dewing, 1722). Map reproduction courtesy of the Norman B. Leventhal Map & Education Center at the Boston Public Library.

cleaned, made and mended clothes, took care of children, gardened, and, by the middle decades of the eighteenth century, did piecework for rapidly expanding industries. They were also fixtures on the streets of New England's towns, going from house to house providing domestic services, hawking goods and buying food in the market, and serving as nurses to the sick.

Chloe Spear was one of these enslaved domestics. Born around 1750 in Africa, she first arrived in Philadelphia during the early 1760s. Soon after arriving, Boston ship captain John Bradford, who was in Pennsylvania on business, purchased the girl and took her home. Spear worked in the Bradford household for the next thirty years in slavery and freedom. In the household, she performed all types of, in the words of her biographer, "domestic duties," including cooking and cleaning. Yet, Spear's work did not confine her to the house. When a neighboring woman fell deathly ill, Spear's mistress sent "her occasionally with a little broth, or with something that might be for the comfort of the individual." Spear, then, pulled double duty as domestic and temporary nurse. Such skills served her well. After being freed in the early 1780s by the Bradfords, Spear and her husband, Caesar Spear, also a freed slave, saved enough money to open their own boardinghouse by 1798. When she died in 1815, Spear had an estate worth over $1,400—a solidly middle-class income for the time.[4]

Chloe Spear was the only domestic owned by the Bradfords, but many enslaved women shared domestic duties with and lived in the same spaces as other bound women. Wealthy Boston merchant Oxenbridge Thatcher dealt in a variety goods, including yarn and thread produced in his home. Spinning yarn was not only women's work but also tedious. Given the monotony, Thatcher's wife and children would have been exempt from performing this work. Who produced all the thread for Thatcher? An examination of his probate inventory reveals that he owned a "Negroe Woman." Yet, this anonymous woman was not the only dependent laboring in Thatcher's household. In 1753, Thatcher received a young female pauper apprentice named Mary Guillion from the Boston Overseers of the Poor. When binding the girl out, they specifically noted that she would learn to be a spinster in the Thatcher household. Teaching her to spin would not be Thatcher or his wife but rather the "Negroe Woman." Thatcher's household demonstrates that not only did women produce valuable items that could be sold outside the home, but householders sought to control many different types of bound female labor, which allowed owners to increase production and, potentially, profits.[5]

Enslaved women were not cloistered inside New England homes. Many were out in the streets, buying and selling goods at the market. They seemed to be effective consumers. In 1728, the town of Boston passed a new law forbidding enslaved people from buying food from farmers and local vendors because they had "inhanced the price of provisions." While the town elders did not clarify or explain why they passed the act, it seems likely that enslaved women were shrewd buyers who proved able to purchase large amounts of food and other goods for lower prices.[6]

In addition to the female domestics, spinsters, and market women, enslaved men also labored in New England's urban households. Often owned by the wealthiest families, these men would be valets, cooks, butlers, carriage drivers, and stablemen. Indeed, their wealthy masters, often times the most politically and economically powerful men in the colony, would dress their enslaved footmen in the latest fashions from Europe. Used not only for their labor but also as a status symbol, these men could be seen accompanying New England's leading families. As early as the 1680s, travelers' accounts record the presence of these men. English visitor Joseph Bennett made special note of how the leading ladies of Boston always had a "negro servant to drive" their carriage when they went out, while the men accompanying the ladies on horse-back always had "their negroes to attend them." They were so commonly beside their masters and mistresses that Bennett took to calling the enslaved African servants of the wealthy their "black equipages."[7]

While many enslaved men toiled in the households of wealthy New Englanders, others more commonly worked beside their masters in workshops or various industrial settings. Bondsmen could be found in nearly every trade and industry in urban New England, supplementing the labor of their masters and, if involved in larger-scale enterprises, their masters' other workers. Enslaved men worked as day laborers, blacksmiths, coopers, masons, carpenters, joiners, caulkers, and in many other occupations. Quite a few of these workers became quite skilled and, while prevented from holding the title, were effectively master craftsmen. Having such skills made slaves valuable contributors to the workforce. Indeed, it was common in urban New England for artisans to purchase young enslaved boys and raise them alongside their own children and apprentices. These boys would grow into men who not only provided additional skilled labor for their master but were also an investment for the family.

Benjamin Eustis Sr. was a carpenter and house builder in early eighteenth-century Boston and serves as a useful example of artisanal slave ownership. We know about his life not from diaries or account books but from the town accounts of Boston. Like urban spaces today, Boston required workers to build, maintain, and repair infrastructure such as roads, bridges, and buildings. Town selectmen would often hire local artisans to complete these tasks. Eustis was one of these con-tractors, taking on six jobs for the town between July and November 1715. Most substantially, he contracted to rebuild the schoolhouse. He completed all the jobs and got paid by the end of November. How? In short, while Eustis was the lead contractor, he had other people working for him, including his brother William. Yet, on the biggest project, the schoolhouse, neither one of the Eustis brothers worked on it very often. Rather, they left it to two enslaved Africans, Daniel, Benjamin's enslaved man, and William's boy, named Joseph. Having Daniel and Joseph rebuild the school allowed Benjamin Eustis to complete the smaller projects and receive more money.[8]

It is fairly self-evident why artisans like Benjamin Eustis would own slaves and put them to work, but what did this work routine mean for Daniel? Beyond his appearance in the town accounts, we know very little about him though we can extrapolate some information. Given how busy the Eustis brothers were with other projects, Daniel apparently worked with Joseph alone on the schoolhouse. Joseph, a boy, would have served Daniel in a similar capacity as an apprentice. The two slaves would have been left to their own devices perhaps with the occasional visit by Benjamin or William to check in on them. What townspeople thought about a black man and boy repairing a school they could never attend is unknown. What we can tell is that Daniel was a skilled carpenter and trusted enough by Eustis to be left alone on a jobsite. Daniel probably enjoyed the autonomy, far from the purview of his master and master's brother, and even had the opportunity to impart his craft to a young man.

Daniel's work also demonstrates how black New Englanders often labored on public works projects. While this occurred in both urban and rural areas, towns, especially major port cities like Boston, were home to many types of public projects directed by town, colonial, and imperial officials. When the British government sent an engineer and directed the colony of Massachusetts to build a fort in Boston Harbor in 1700, for example, the colony hired enslaved craftsmen. Likewise, enslaved men labored at Boston's Townhouse (today's Old State House), the seat of the colonial and imperial government in Massachusetts, during its construction, and continued repairing it until the end of slavery. Even free blacks were expected to labor on public works as they were barred from bearing arms and serving in the militia. Towns like Boston calculated the number of days free black men were to repair roads and bridges based off the days a white man would have militia duty.

Needless to say, enslaved workers could be found laboring on projects in public and private capacities across New England's towns. Perhaps where their contributions were most visible, however, were in the industries that kept New England's economic engine running, most importantly, shipbuilding and distilling. The region was a center of shipbuilding with Boston leading the way. By 1690, Boston was the second largest shipbuilding center in the British Empire. And Boston was only one of many New England shipbuilding centers, albeit the largest. Salem and Plymouth, Massachusetts; New London, Connecticut; and Newport and Bristol, Rhode Island, also had numerous shipyards. Building a ship was a labor-intensive process requiring more than thirty trades to complete the work. Over the course of the eighteenth century, New England's shipyards became increasingly reliant on enslaved labor as production expanded. Slaves provided both skilled and unskilled labor, although they often performed the most dangerous work. The historical record reflects this pattern. An enslaved caulker high on the stern of a ship under construction in December 1748 slipped and fell onto a wood pile below, instantly killing him.[9] Nevertheless, slaves were vital to shipbuilding, both supplementing the white labor force and providing their own skills and expertise.

Distilling was another major industry in New England by the early eighteenth century. Using molasses acquired from the Caribbean, New Englanders distilled rum, which they consumed at home and sold abroad. Rhode Island in particular was a major site of rum production, as the beverage was the most important trade commodity Rhode Islanders used to purchase captives in Africa. By the early 1770s, Newport had more than twenty distilleries. Many employed enslaved workers, and distillers were often some of the largest slave owners in New England. Boston distillers, for example, owned on average more than 2 slaves, while the average for Bostonians as a whole was 1.75.

Like shipbuilding, however, distilling was dangerous work. Newspapers are replete with horror stories of the dangers of distillation. On 25 August 1735, the *Boston Evening Post* reported that a slave belonging to distiller Isaac White, while carrying "high Wines from the Still," tripped and fell, splashing the liquor onto himself and an open flame in the still house. The liquid quickly ignited, setting the enslaved man alight. He "ran into the Sea to quench himself" but later died of his burns.[10] Distilleries were dangerous sites of production, and given the high costs of free labor, it was difficult for distillers to find enough workers. They turned to slaves and in turn exposed them to hazard.

Enslaved workers could also be found in more specialized urban labor. Often confined to the largest and most cosmopolitan towns—namely Boston and Newport—these included clock-making, gold- and silver-smithing, and printing. Almost every eighteenth-century Boston printer owned slaves. They helped maintain the shop, set type, and circulate printed works. We know of one of these enslaved men, named Peter Fleet, from the record he left behind. Fleet labored in the workshop of his master, printer Thomas Fleet. Isaiah Thomas, a Boston-born printer and first historian of printing in the early United States, in his *History of Printing in in America,* recalled meeting Peter Fleet while completing his own apprenticeship. Fleet, according to Thomas, was an "ingenious man, and cut, on wooden blocks, all the pictures which decorated the ballads and small books of his master."[11] Indeed, in Thomas Fleet's edition of the English novel *The Prodigal Daughter,* Peter carved the woodcut for the title page and even left his initials, "P. F," for all to see. Working in such a highly specialized field and mastering that craft allowed Peter Fleet to leave his mark on society in a very literal way.

Large numbers of enslaved men in New England also worked onboard ships as sailors and support staff. Most of them would have resided in the region's port cities, and historians have estimated that a quarter of the enslaved men who lived in the coastal areas of Massachusetts worked on the water. Some of these men would have worked on ferries, transporting goods and people around New England's waterways. Others would have labored on small boats called lighters, which were used to move goods locally. Many also staffed the deep-water vessels that plied the Atlantic Ocean, meaning that many enslaved men traveled far from New England and visited Europe, the Caribbean, and other parts of North America.

Lucky for us, there are many records of enslaved sailors from eighteenth-century New England that document their lives. Numerous slaves, much like those in the trades, started young, often learning the rudiments of sailing from their masters. One of the few documents

The Prodigal Daughter:

Or a ftrange and wonderful Relation, Shewing how a
Gentleman of a vaft Eftate in *Briftol*, had a proud and dif-
obedient Daughter, who, becaufe her Parents would not
fupport her in all her Extravagance, bargained with the
Devil to poifon them.——How an Angel informed her Parents
of her Defign.——How fhe lay in a Trance four Days; and
when fhe was put in the Grave, fhe came to Life again, and
related the wounderful Things fhe faw in the other World.
Likewife the Subftance of a Sermon preach'd on this Occa-
fion by the Rev. Mr. *Williams*, from *Lu* XV, 24.

Sold at the Heart and Crown, in Cornhill, *Bofton.*

FIGURE 8. Peter Fleet's woodcut cover of *The Prodigal Daughter Revived* (1736;
reprint, Boston: Thomas Fleet, ca. 1750). Note the initials "P. F" at the bottom. ©
President and Fellows of Harvard College. Harvard Art Museums/Fogg Museum,
Gift of Rona Schneider.

regarding the training of enslaved workers in New England actually comes from an indenture copied into a Boston notary's account book. In October 1760, Caesar, a slave who belonged to ship captain Peter McTaggart, "of his own free will" apprenticed himself to his master in order to learn how to sail. Why McTaggart had Caesar—his own property—enter a formal apprenticeship remains a mystery, but it provides a record that the slave had seafaring experience and was thus more valuable than an unskilled slave. It is doubtful that there was any "free will" involved but rather the desire of McTaggart to invest in his enslaved property.[12]

Once trained, enslaved sailors took to the seas. Life for them would have been similar to white sailors hoisting the sails, cleaning the decks, manning the pumps, and making repairs. In addition, slaves often filled ancillary roles, such as serving as the ship's cook—many times in addition to their regular duties as a seaman. They made similar wages to other sailors, although a portion of that would be remitted to their masters. Often confined to merchant ships, which were notoriously understaffed by ship owners and investors looking to save money, bound sailors had the opportunity to explore the world and enjoy a degree of autonomy far away from the prying eyes of masters, town and colonial officials, and others looking to police their behavior. Traveling from port to port around the Atlantic also placed these New Englanders in an important social position. Having learned the latest news and gossip on their travels, they were vital in the transmission and dissemination of information among the enslaved and marginalized populations.

Perhaps the most famous enslaved New England sailor was Briton Hammon. We know of Hammon today because in 1760, he published a narrative of his thirteen-year misadventure entitled *A Narrative of the Uncommon Sufferings and Surprizing Deliverance of Briton Hammon.* While Hammon embellished much of his story, it still provides a fascinating glimpse at the lives of men who were both sailors and slaves. Hammon was from Marshfield, Massachusetts, and in 1747 joined the crew of a ship headed to Jamaica and the Mosquito Coast (modern-day Nicaragua and Honduras) to harvest logwood. On the return trip, the ship ran aground in the Florida Keys. These islands were in territory claimed by Spain, a nation with little patience for New England inter-lopers. Local Native Americans were the first to encounter the ship-wreck. Allies of Spain, the Indians ambushed the crew, killing everyone save Hammon. It seems Hammon's black skin saved his life as the Natives correctly assumed he was a slave and knew they could sell him to the Spanish for money. They sold Hammon to a passing Spanish ship captain, who then took him to the Spanish island of Cuba. There, the governor general of the colony purchased Hammon and put him to work in his household. After a year of service, the governor desired to hire Hammon out to a Spanish merchant ship, but the slave refused. For his intransigence, he spent four years in a dark Cuban prison. Upon his release, the bishop of Havana hired Hammon to carry him around the countryside on a litter. Sick of drudgery and dungeons, Hammon encountered an English smuggler in Havana, who put him onboard his ship to Jamaica. From there, he secured passage to London, working on the ship to pay his way. He then found a ship to Boston where, once onboard, he magically encountered his master, one General Winslow, who was happy to see his bondsman.[13]

Hammon's narrative is certainly exceptional, and there are good reasons to doubt its authenticity. Nevertheless, it demonstrates two important facts about enslaved New England sailors. First, Hammon's skills were valuable and vital. As an experienced sailor in a world where maritime labor was expensive and dear, he was able to use those skills to negotiate passage and get himself out of sticky situations. Indeed, the only time he received punishment during his Cuban captivity was when he withheld those skills and refused to sail. Likewise, Hammon's narra-tive gives us a sense of just how extensively these men traveled. While not everyone spent thirteen years abroad, many did have long itineraries. They visited distant ports and experienced much of the Atlantic first-hand. These experiences would have ultimately allowed them to better understand their own position in the world and how to navigate more successfully their enslavement.

Rural Places

Although most enslaved New Englanders lived in and around the region's major urban areas, many lived in rural areas. While the incidence of slave ownership was usually much lower, enslaved people were still nearly everywhere in rural New England. Indeed, some places, such as Rhode Island's Narragansett Country, had large numbers of slaves living there. Even towns far removed from Boston and Newport, such as Deerfield, Massachusetts, could host large numbers of enslaved people. Deerfield, situated in the fertile Connecticut River Valley, was home to twenty-five slaves in 1752. Given that only three hundred people lived in Deerfield, that meant slaves, nearly all of them African, comprised 8 percent of the town's population, a proportion slightly lower than that of Boston. In other towns, especially poor frontier areas, there may have only been one or two enslaved people. Thus, much like New England's urban slaves, rural slaves would have performed myriad tasks and worked a variety of jobs from subsistence farming to artisanal work to large-scale agricultural and livestock production. Once again, labor was gendered, but women could be found working in the fields alongside men and were vital to large-scale production. To understand enslaved labor in rural New England, it is best to turn to case studies to explore the variety of labor arrangements and working conditions.

In September 1727, New London justice of the peace, landowner, carpenter, farmer, and diarist Joshua Hempstead was assessing the estate of a recently deceased neighbor, Samuel Fox. Trusted by local officials, Hempstead meticulously appraised Fox's belongings, including a young enslaved man named Adam Jackson. About twenty-seven years old, Jackson had spent the better part of his life as a slave in the Fox household, despite both of his parents having been freed. As Hempstead assessed his neighbor's belongings, he got to know Jackson, and ultimately, on 26 September, purchased the enslaved man for eighty-five pounds. Jackson commanded such a high price because he was a native of New England, familiar with its history, traditions, and peculiar labor system. He had honed his skills in husbandry and was widely regarded as a dutiful bondsman. Until Hempstead's death in 1758, Jackson would be his slave, providing valuable labor for his master's many economic endeavors.

Although New London was a booming port town, it was still deeply connected to its rural hinterland. Many residents, including Hempstead, lived with a foot in both worlds, and Hempstead engaged in overseas commerce, worked as a carpenter and shipbuilder on the waterfront, and farmed. Jackson likewise labored in two worlds, often working outside the purview of Hempstead, who as a justice of the peace and merchant traveled for days at a time. Jackson performed many types of work, including loading goods onto ships in the New London dockyards and carting goods around town. Yet, he spent most of his days working on Hempstead's farm in Stonington, Connecticut, and harvesting hay in the area's salt marshes. On the farm, he planted a variety of crops and tended the fields. He spent a significant amount of his time working with the livestock, especially Hempstead's large flock of sheep but also sizable herds of cattle, pigs, and oxen. Jackson drove them to different pastures, rounded them up, gelded the young males, and slaughtered them at various times of the year. He understood the animals and kept order on the farm. Hempstead, for example, owned—perhaps "stuck with" being a more operative term—one team of oxen that "no one will Keep them [because] they are So unruley," but Jackson had no issues driving them. In short, he was a skilled and excellent husbandman.

With skills came autonomy and power. Jackson worked on the Stonington farm with little supervision, although Hempstead would occasionally check in on him. Jackson's work also often took him off the farm when he needed to cart goods to market. A capable driver—as the example of the oxen demonstrates—Jackson became a trusted delivery-man around town, not only taking Hempstead's produce to market but carting goods for others too. While Jackson did work on his own, it is unclear if he got to keep any of his wages or had to remit them all to Hempstead. Yet, he accrued power and social capital in other ways. His skills brought him respect in the community, and thus he did not raise suspicions in the way other people of African descent would have when out on the street or interacting with fellow townspeople. Even more significantly, Jackson was in many ways the master of the Stonington farm, sometimes quite literally. The size of the farm meant at certain times of year, Jackson could not complete all the necessary work on his own. Hempstead would hire local boys, other slaves, and Indians to work on the farm who were all subject to Jackson's management. Like so much in his life, he proved a capable and effective supervisor.[14]

Adam Jackson represented one type of rural slave labor in New England, but there were other forms. In the fertile Connecticut River Valley in both Connecticut and Massachusetts, for example, many of the towns came to hold relatively large slave populations. As mentioned, Deerfield, a bustling farming community by the 1750s, had a sizable slave population. Much like New London, however, Deerfield straddled two worlds. Rather than being both rural and urban, Deerfield was both on the frontier and a wealthy farming community. Subject to multiple raids by the French and their Native American allies during the eighteenth century, Deerfield was also stable enough to host large, lucrative farms, many of which employed slave labor.

By 1752, twenty-five enslaved people lived in Deerfield. Six were women and girls; nineteen were men and boys, demonstrating that the need for workers in the field outweighed that for domestic vocations. Nevertheless, the lives of these rural enslaved women give us insight into the working worlds of those enslaved in Deerfield. One of these women was Jinny, who belonged to Deerfield's second minister, Jonathan Ashley. To better understand Jinny's life, it is important to examine slave ownership outside of New England's urban centers. While most slave owners in rural areas were farmers, many of them were older, like Joshua Hempstead, when they acquired their bondspeople for the first time. They used a lifetime's worth of savings to purchase slaves to help around the house and in the fields once their children were gone. Likewise, some of the leading slaveholders in rural New England were ministers, like Ashley, who, as integral members of New England's social fabric, had the connections necessary to acquire enslaved people. Ashley purchased Jinny in Boston, most likely because, despite living far away in the Connecticut River Valley, he had associations with Boston's ecclesiastical, commercial, and social circles.

Despite Ashley's cosmopolitan contacts, Jinny's labor reflected life on New England's frontier. We have few records of Jinny, but there is an interesting reference to her working life. Jinny died in 1808, long after the end of slavery in Massachusetts, but she still lived with Ashley's widow, Dorothy, and worked as a domestic until the end of her days. Shortly before her death, a neighbor recorded seeing Jinny and Dorothy "sitting together busily engaged in sewing."[15] Despite being long after the end of her servitude, this is the type of labor Jinny and many women, free and bound, in rural New England performed. While the enslaved men of Deerfield lived similar lives to Adam Jackson, women mostly worked in the home, sewing and mending clothes. Deerfield was far removed from places manufacturing cloth and clothing, leaving it up to either women or local tailors, who were in short supply, charged high rates, and often engaged in other work. Thus, enslaved women like Jinny were vital fixtures of New England's rural economy. Outside of providing some auxiliary farm labor, their work was largely invisible and does not appear in account books of commercial transactions or receipts for goods received. Rather, it was a silent economy, one that freed the men—free and enslaved—to tend fields and expand dominion over the frontier.

Having enslaved domestics like Jinny to support male laborers made sense in rural areas with great soil like Deerfield, but other, less fertile areas tended to only support a few slaves to work the fields. A good example of this type of slavery comes from the diary of Ebenezer Parkman of Westborough, Massachusetts. Shortly after completing his degree and training as a minister, in 1721 Parkman became the first permanent minister of Westborough. Although settled in the 1670s, the town only became fully incorporated in 1717. Life in this new town would have been hard for all the settlers and especially for Parkman. He was a Bostonian by birth and the son of a tradesman with little clue about the rigors of farming in rural Worcester County.

Perhaps his ignorance of farming and rural life inspired him to look for additional help around the farm. In spring 1728, Parkman's brother Elias, a mast-maker living in the North End of Boston, hosted slave trader Henry Richards. Richards used Elias's home to sell a "likely parcel of negro boys and one negro girl," who arrived from Africa via the island of Nevis in the Caribbean. The Parkmans' father apparently purchased one of the boys, named Maro, because in August 1728, Ebenezer Parkman purchased Maro from his father on credit for seventy-four pounds. Soon after, Parkman returned to Westborough hoping to put

Maro (sometimes called Barrow) to work. Maro appeared infrequently in Parkman's diary, but at first he seemed to be a good servant, dutifully accompanying the minister on his travels around the countryside.

Purchasing a slave was not a panacea, however. On 27 August 1728, Parkman, who should have been preparing his weekly sermon, had to stay home and help the family around the farm. He complained that "our Negro being New" failed to address his family's "want of Help" and caused him to be "taken off from my Work" as a minister. Nevertheless, Parkman trusted "in God it may be better with me and more leasure ere long." For Parkman, slave ownership was an effective way of relieving the strains of frontier living, but that relief would take time and additional work to train Maro. And relief never came. In December 1728, less than six months after purchasing the boy, Parkman made an ominous entry in his diary. "Dark as it has been with us," the minister recorded, "it became much Darker abt ye Sun Setting. The Sun of Maro's life Sat. The first Death in my Family!"[16] As with many new arrivals from Africa, Maro died shortly after his arrival in the Americas. Parkman's diary demonstrates how this was a devastating blow for his household in more ways than just losing a laborer.

While Parkman purchased a single slave to eke out a living in a newly established town, other areas, such as Narragansett Country, were home to large slave labor forces and intensive, export-oriented agriculture. The Narragansett Country, also called South County, home of Reverend MacSparran, was a fertile area of land in southwestern Rhode Island that spilled into eastern Connecticut. This region had rich soil, fertile grasslands, and a much more temperate climate than the rest of New England. Those factors, combined with easy access to Newport, Bristol, and New London, made the Narragansett Country perfect for large-scale agriculture. Although most of the farmers who lived there owned fewer than five slaves, a number of large landowners, who owned more than ten bondsmen and -women, cultivated the area. In that sense, South County resembled the southern colonies of Virginia, North Carolina, and South Carolina, where small farmers with few slaves lived alongside great planters with many. Beyond living around yeomen, the lives of the wealthiest Narragansett planters resembled those of southern and Caribbean planters in other ways. They built their homes in the style of

English manor houses, commissioned portraits of themselves and their families, and controlled politics in the region. They even intermarried to consolidate their control, landholdings, and wealth.

Underpinning this lifestyle were large, especially by New England standards, slave holdings. While planters still relied on Indian day laborers and white indentured servants, enslaved Africans came to dominate the labor force. Many of these slaves came directly from Africa via Rhode Island's slave trade. By the 1750s, a third of the people living in South County were enslaved, and the area hosted the densest population of slaves in New England. The great planters owned more than ten slaves each, with some, such as Robert Hazard, allegedly owning more than forty. Unlike plantations elsewhere, the Narragansett Country did not produce a lucrative cash crop like tobacco or sugar. Rather, they took advantage of the fertile land to raise vast herds of livestock and maintain diversified farms that produced foodstuffs for export.

Most important to these operations were the livestock. Narragansett planters raised cattle and horses for dairy, meat, and export. Most of these commodities went to the West Indies and American South, where cash crop agriculture precluded raising livestock. In terms of dairy, the South County produced large amounts of cheese. Hazard owned more than 1,600 acres of land, which was home to more than 100 cattle. With those resources, Hazard's farm produced more than 13,000 pounds (by weight) of cheese annually. To do that, Hazard relied on a workforce of "twelve negro women as dairy women, each of whom had a girl to assist her."[17] While the author of this quotation may have exaggerated the number of enslaved women Hazard had working for him, the comment still demonstrates how the planter depended on the labor of enslaved women to produce sufficient quantities of cheese for export. As the women labored away milking cattle and making cheese, the enslaved men of the Narragansett Country were cowboys par excellence. They rustled cattle, sheared sheep, and shoed horses. Others were skilled blacksmiths and carpenters, providing vital support to the cowboys. And it was a wild success. Narragansett planters, no matter how hard they tried, could not meet their Caribbean counterparts' demands for cattle to operate mills and horses to ride, and white colonists in South County became increasingly reliant on enslaved labor.

By the early eighteenth century, enslaved people could be found work-ing everywhere in New England, from the region's largest town, Boston, to rural, frontier areas such as Maine. New Englanders had created a booming, export-oriented economy, but it was both a blessing and a curse. Surely, it generated wealth, but to continue to build that wealth, colonists had to address a serious shortage of labor. They ultimately settled on using slave labor. While labor shortages were common across the Americas in the seventeenth and eighteenth centuries, the way New Englanders deployed slave labor was unique. They largely attempted to adapt slavery into their traditional labor practices centered around households and household production. Thus, while the wealthy did own slaves, the largest number of slave owners were actually farmers and tradesmen looking to incorporate more labor into their house-holds. Slaves were valuable investments for New England families, ones that appreciated over time and could be sold.

Slavery, then, was an adaptation white New Englanders made to the realities of the labor market. New Englanders incorporated enslaved men and women into their unique labor system, which also meant they were active enslavers and used the most common form of bound labor in the early Americas. Being part of a local manifestation of a transna-tional institution, enslaved men and women became important fixtures in the region's labor market. While the value of slave labor helped fur-ther transform them into a commodity—a thing that could be bought and sold—it also offered some protections and opportunities, such as the ability to self-hire and earn wages. Laboring beside tradesmen, goodwives, and farmers also meant enslaved New Englanders acquired valuable skills that could serve them in various ways. Finally, it helped to foster associations with fellow workers and gave slaves an excuse to be out on the streets and about town. Wages could be used to better slaves' lives, even if only in material ways. The work enslaved people performed was inherently tied to the families they created, communi-ties they fostered, and the resistance they mustered against slavery.

CHAPTER 5

KIN AND COMMUNITY

E NSLAVED PEOPLE IN New England created families, fostered communities, and developed strategies to resist and challenge their enslavement. Despite the odds, they made friends, partook in public celebrations, and gathered with other marginalized men and women for rest and relaxation. Most importantly, although slaves may not have envisioned it as such, all these activities helped to subvert and reshape the institution of slavery. In theory, enslaved people, by virtue of being the property of another, were cut off from society except through their enslavers. This concept, called "social death" by historians and social scientists, means that enslaved people had no individual will and masters were in total control. Social death alienated enslaved people from society at large and caused others to regard them as not fully human.

This concept reflects the letter of the law and popular attitudes, however, rather than reality. Enslaved New Englanders engaged in certain acts, such as forming families, forging friendships, participating in communal activities, and affiliating with local institutions, that challenged the idea of social death. These activities provided space for enslaved men and women to express their humanity. More to the point, enslaved people found direct ways of challenging their enslavement, from various strategies to get out of work to running away to violence and open rebellion.

Family Life

Despite many obstacles, enslaved people in New England formed families. Like others, they courted, held marriage ceremonies, and had children. Family formation among New England's slaves was a contested act across multiple fronts. Men, often comprising a majority of the enslaved population, especially in the port cities, had to compete for women. Separation from spouses and the demands of enslavement could drive a wedge into the happiest of marriages. Most importantly, masters had to consent to partnerships and could sell children away for their own economic gain or as punishment. Nevertheless, the records of slavery in New England do allow us to see the process of family formation. In addition to this process, however, it is important to look at the diversity of familial relations among enslaved people in early New England.

Three larger factors shaped enslaved marriages. First, enslaved Native Americans and Africans conceived of marriage differently than white New Englanders. Since most slaves in eighteenth-century New England were African, we can look to experiences there. In Africa, marriage was often a communal consideration where the families of the potential bride and groom would meet and discuss the nature of the union. Given that most enslaved Africans did not arrive in the Americas as a family unit, such discussions would have been impossible and left "sexual desire" in place of "long-term considerations of compatibility." Even more troubling for white observers was the African practice of polygamy. It was common for men to marry multiple women in Africa, and the practice traveled across the Atlantic. New Englanders, however, practiced and demanded monogamy, foisting a particular vision of marriage on enslaved people.[1]

Second, although bound Africans and Indians may have had different conceptions of marriage than white New Englanders, colonial authorities wanted slaves to marry in the New England fashion. Encouragement can most clearly be seen in Massachusetts, where in 1705, the colony passed a law permitting enslaved people the right to marry. Even though slave marriages were not explicitly legal in the other New England colonies, slaves still had access to church marriages. The numerous banns, or announcements, for enslaved marriages demonstrate the popularity of this option. In Little Compton, Rhode Island, Congregational minister Richard Billings recorded the "intent of marriage between Cesar negro servant to Nathaniel Church and Sarah negro servant to John Pabodie" on 11 September 1731. Billings married the couple on 7 October of that same year.[2] The case of Cesar and Sarah also demonstrates the centrality of ministers in small towns and major port cities in encouraging marriage. Between the law and ecclesiastical encouragements, legal, formalized slave marriages had a strong foundation in New England.

Finally, gender ratios and the population density of slaves across the region affected marriage rates. In many towns, including the largest port cities such as Boston and Salem, enslaved men far outnumbered enslaved women. Solid demographic figures are hard to compile, although tax returns and censuses (also used for taxation) give us some idea. Most useful is a 1754 census from Massachusetts that calculated the number of slaves living there. While the data the colony produced is problematic, because masters would often hide enslaved people since they were taxable property, a clear trend emerges. Of the 102 towns that reported slaves to the Massachusetts legislature, 75, or nearly 74 percent, reported more male slaves than female ones. Some of these figures were quite dramatic. Medford, Massachusetts, for example, contained thirty-three male slaves and only ten women.[3] Likewise, in rural areas, there were often only a handful of enslaved people in the region. Both the preponderance of men and the relatively low population density of enslaved people were significant barriers to family formation.

These larger factors—different conceptions of marriage, encouragement of matrimony by authorities, and demographic issues—shaped the process of family formation in early New England. In no place can that be seen more clearly than in courtship practices. Unless enslaved men and women had the same master, there were many obstacles to courtship. Laws circumscribing slave behavior, such as curfews and limits on alcohol consumption, limited opportunities to fraternize. Likewise, the demands of work, especially for women, who often worked in their masters' homes, hindered meeting a potential partner. Nevertheless, enslaved people, as we see below, were members of communal organizations such as churches, defied restrictions such as the curfew, and, based on the complaints of masters and white neighbors, socialized with one another outside of working hours. These spaces and moments created opportunities for meeting a spouse.

That said, the evidence concerning courtship does suggest fierce competition among men looking for mates, likely due to the skewed gender ratio. Court records, for example, document duels and other affairs of honor between enslaved men. For instance, Quaco, an enslaved African man brought to New England from the Dutch colony of Suriname, stood accused in 1762 of poisoning another slave named Boston, who later died. When authorities investigated the murder, they interviewed James and Sarah Gardiner, the owner of an enslaved man named Sambo. According to the Gardiners, Quaco was angry with Boston because the latter had sided with Sambo in a dispute. Sambo and Quaco "had Quarrelled and fought about a Negro woman they were acquainted with." In addition to alleging that Quaco poisoned Boston, the Gardiners claimed that he had also poisoned some hogs that belonged to Sambo. Both acts were "in revenge to Sambo."[4]

A much less dramatic way of finding a mate can be seen in the actions of Sampson, an enslaved man living in the town of Canterbury, New Hampshire. Sampson belonged to Archelaus Moore. At some point, Sampson decided he wanted to marry, but living in Canterbury, a remote town on New England's frontier, he was perhaps the only slave living there. For that reason, he turned to the nearest settlement of any size, Concord, New Hampshire. There he met Lucy, an enslaved woman who belonged to one of Concord's leading men, William Coffin. Sampson "wanted her for his wife." Distance between Canterbury and Concord would have created problems for any relationship. So Sampson agreed to work for Coffin for one year in exchange for Lucy. Moore must also have been involved in this process. He probably consented to Sampson working for Coffin. In exchange, he would receive Lucy and any children born to her and Sampson. It would have also better ensured Sampson's happiness and meant he would not run away to Concord to see his wife.[5]

Sampson's case was not an isolated one, as many enslaved and free black men in New England purchased enslaved women as their wives.

While purchasing a wife was certainly not a New England custom or a common form of courtship for whites, it nevertheless made sense to people of African descent. It not only matched African customs of paying a wife's family but it also ensured that black men could find a spouse. How the women felt about this arrangement, however, is unknown.

No matter how enslaved men and women courted one another, marriage soon followed. Slave marriages fell under the same laws as white marriages, meaning couples had to announce their intentions to marry, as the law considered marriage a civil as opposed to religious act, and their ceremonies had to be conducted by ministers and magistrates, many of them the leading men of the colonies. Slavery intruded on almost every facet of the act of marriage. Andover, Massachusetts, minister Samuel Phillips, for example, created his own vows for slaves he married titled "A Form for a *Negroe-Marriage*." While the vows between the betrothed were similar to those of whites, Phillips added two addenda at the end specifically for enslaved people. He first made the couple attest that their marriage was "with the consent of [their] Masters and Mistresses." Then, he added an entire clause reminding the couple that they "remain still, and truly as ever," their "Master's property," and thus it was "justly expected" that they would "behave and conduct" themselves "as Obedient and faithfull Servants."[6] Phillips echoed the sentiments of colonial officials and masters across the region. Matrimony came second to mastery.

Indeed, masters and mistresses often meddled in the love lives of their slaves. Reverend Stephen Williams of Longmeadow, Massachusetts, owned a number of slaves throughout his life, including an enslaved woman named Phillis. Williams kept a detailed diary of his everyday life and documented his interactions with his family, free and enslaved. Phillis announced her intentions to marry in early 1738. Although Williams does not record who she was to marry, the minister seemed to be in favor of the prospect. Nevertheless, while Williams encouraged marriage, his wife was "so averse." This predicament put the minister "in a Strait." He must have eventually sided with his wife because Phillis did not marry until six years later in 1744.[7] Marriage for enslaved people was not easy once they overcame the difficulties of courtship.

Rather, and despite encouragement from colonial and religious officials, masters and mistresses often attempted to undermine slave marriages.

Children were an important part of this family formation. Many enslaved couples had children, both in and out of wedlock. There is little documentation regarding how enslaved people raised their children, and much of what does exist concerns mothers and children. Such attention to this relationship can be explained by New England's concern with enslaved people being property. Acknowledging which slave child belonged to which enslaved woman proved the status of the child, thus marking them as property. While meant to demarcate property relations, it allows us to see the relationship between enslaved women and their children.

A good example of this mother-child bond was that of Jinny, a woman we met last chapter who was by the prominent Ashley family of Deerfield, Massachusetts. Jinny was from the kingdom of the Kongo in West Central Africa and allegedly the "daughter of a king." When she was about twelve years old in the mid-1730s, she and some other children were playing near a well. A "gang of white villains" ambushed the group, bound them, and rushed them onboard a slave ship. It was rare for whites to conduct their own slaving raids on the African coast. During this time, however, the Kongo was in a period of prolonged civil war. Kongolese authority would have been weak and unable to police the actions of unscrupulous slave traders. These white "villains" were also New Englanders. They would not have had the connections to Kongolese slave traders and may have conducted their own raids out of desperation. Regardless, the slavers kidnapped Jinny and sold her in Boston where Jonathan Ashley, Deerfield's minister, purchased the little girl.

Family proved to be a cornerstone of Jinny's life. Years after being kidnapped and having a child of her own, someone in Deerfield asked about her capture. Telling the story of playing by the well and the "white villains," she lamented that after being placed onboard the ship, "we nebber see our mudders [mothers] any more." As a mother, Jinny's sorrow of being ripped away from her own haunted her for the rest of her life.

Jinny had a son named Cato. Little is known about Cato's birthdate or father, although Jonathan Ashley baptized the child in 1739. As a native of Africa and a noblewoman at that, Jinny never fully acclimated to life in New England and passed many of her customs onto her son. Most importantly, as with many other enslaved Africans in the Americas, Jinny believed on her death that she would cross the ocean and return to her homeland. She prepared "all kinds of odds and ends" for her final passage, most likely hoping to return with the material wealth in accordance to her status. Jinny passed on these customs to Cato. When he died in 1825, the Ashleys discovered he had "gathered trinkets to provide for his transition."[8] Enslaved parents valued family and childrearing, nurtured their children the best they could, and shared important knowledge and traditions with their children.

Nevertheless, much like marriage, the property rights of slaveholders had the potential to destroy families and rip children away from their parents. Enslaved people were valuable property in New England and could easily be sold for cash or to cover debts. Given the fact that so many farmers and tradesmen preferred to raise enslaved children in their households, younger slaves were especially salable. For Juno Larcom, an enslaved woman in Beverly, Massachusetts, this situation was all too real. Her master, David Larcom, owed interest on a loan. To cover the payments, he sold three of Juno's children and eventually her husband. Cold, calculated economic decisions of the master class decimated families.

Harrowing accounts of families destroyed by sale haunt the records of every slave society, but there was a particular cruel practice exclusive to New England. Regional newspapers are full of advertisements such as the following: "A fine Negro child, of a good healthy breed to be given away."[9] New England masters commonly gave enslaved children away to others once their mothers had weaned them. A number of factors help to explain this phenomenon, notably the nature of slaveholding in the region. Given that most enslaved people lived with middling families of farmers and tradesmen, the birth of a child created two interrelated problems from the owner's point of view. First, the child, especially once weaned, was another mouth to feed in homes already on tight budgets and stretched thin. It should be no surprise, then, that giving away enslaved children increased during economic downturns. Second, childrearing, especially of an infant and toddler, distracted the mother, meaning she could not focus entirely on her own work. The practice occurred for other reasons as well. It could help cover up the sexual transgressions of the master or his sons, which would be more noticeable in a society with small slaveholding. Finally, farmers and tradesmen preferred young people to serve as slaves where they could be raised in their households. Receiving a free child would go a long way in achieving that goal.

Economic motives undermined the slave family in New England, but mothers and fathers did resist attempts to stymie the economic imperatives of the master class. Many sought to build a family with little regard to the prerogatives of the master. The story of Silvia, an enslaved woman who lived in New Haven, Connecticut, proves instructive. She made her daughter, Hagar, follow a strict code of conduct. When white women requested Hagar dance for them, for example, Silvia forbade the child from accepting money. Silvia most likely sought to teach her daughter to not accept rewards for humiliating herself. Likewise, Silvia ordered Hagar to never refer to the house they shared with their master as "home." Home was a life created apart from the owner, where Hagar and Silvia could enjoy their relationship away from their enslaver. Finally, when their owner threatened Silvia with separation from Hagar, the mother informed the master that she would "spill her last drop of blood" to prevent her daughter from being sold away. The master demurred.[10]

Marriages and family formation were not always formalized and solemnized. Enslaved men and women frequently formed lasting, loving relationships and had children outside of wedlock. Indeed, it happened so often that whites came to call this practice "Negro marriage." A number of factors explain the frequency of these types of unions. As mentioned, many enslaved people in New England were Africans or Native Americans from communities that practiced polygamy. More casual "marriages" allowed men to have multiple partners without raising the ire of authorities. Likewise, "Negro marriages" were an important way of dealing with the prerogatives of the master class. If two enslaved people married officially and one was sold away, the spouse left behind would have to go through the process of getting a divorce if he or she wanted to remarry. In the eighteenth century, that required a resolve from the colonial legislature—no easy task. For that reason, many couples, such as Juno Larcom mentioned above, would build a solid relationship and have children—Larcom had four—before solemnizing their marriages.

In addition to these informal marriages, many enslaved people married across status and racial lines. Some enslaved men married free black women. These relationships suggest a generational calculation where the men might not become free but any children they had would be. It was also common for free black men to marry enslaved women, often times purchasing them directly. These relationships could be coercive, as the story of a Warwick, Rhode Island, freedman named Boston Carpenter attests. During the American Revolution, Carpenter purchased an enslaved woman named Lill. While Carpenter never married Lill, he also never freed her. That gave him considerable power over his partner, and he would reputedly often tell her that "if she did not behave well, he would put her in his pocket (or, in other words, he would sell her)."[11]

Beyond cross-status relationships, many enslaved people married across the racial barrier. Although prohibited by law, enslaved Africans and Indians formed relationships with whites. As discussed in chapter 3, many white men sexually exploited enslaved women. Other liaisons between whites and people of color could be more loving, however. A Boston court convicted an enslaved African man named Cesar of fornicating with a white woman, Mary Goslin, in 1705. Before the prosecution, Cesar and Mary had a child, which is what drew the attention of the authorities. Sentenced to be whipped for his crime, Cesar challenged the court, "behaved himself impudently," and refused to accept the punishment. He informed the court that he "would be again guilty of the same crime." For his insubordination, the slave received an additional twenty-five lashes from the court.[12] Nevertheless, his defiance demonstrates how enslaved people could have loving, committed relationships with whites. Cesar's desire to maintain a relationship with Goslin despite the punishment shows how enslaved people in the region asserted their desire to form relationships and families on their own terms.

While all the New England colonies banned relationships between people of African and Indian descent and whites, there were no laws prohibiting those two groups from intermarrying. By the end of the colonial period, it was common for enslaved African men to marry free Indian women. Numerous documents attest to this phenomenon, including one runaway slave advertisement from Portsmouth, Rhode Island. In 1741, Robert Lawton reported that his "portly young Mollatto fellow" ran away "and had with him an Indian Squaw which he called his Wife."[13]

Why would this man be so ready to abscond with an Indian woman? There were many factors driving intermarriage, including demographics. Much as African men outnumbered African women in New England, Indian women outnumbered Indian men. After the colonies subjugated the indigenous population in southern New England following King Philip's War in 1676, the colonies required the men to serve. These obligations often required military service, meaning Indian men fought and died in the many British wars against the French between 1689 and 1763. Moreover, Indian men also disproportionately served as sailors, especially on New England whaling ships, which paid good money regardless of race. Some of these men never returned home from their voyages.

Demographics were not destiny, however, and the generational calculation also drove this intermixture. Most Indian women, especially those who lived on reservations in rural parts of southern New England, were free and had claims to tribal land. Any children they bore for their enslaved husbands would likewise be free and have access to land. Being born free property owners was a far cry from their father's status and could make interracial marriage appealing.

Community

Even as enslaved people formed families with other people of color, they also formed communal structures. Communities for enslaved New Englanders, however, did not resemble those of other slave societies in the Americas. Rare were large slaveholdings in a region mostly populated by small farmers and tradesmen. The majority of slaves lived one or two to a household, often in isolated, rural areas. Community, then, had a different meaning. Instead of thinking of a racially exclusive slave community, it is better to think in terms of association. Enslaved people associated with many different people and institutions in New England, which they used to leverage various advantages and material benefits. That is not to imply that all association was instrumental. Rather, enslaved people in New England were intentional about who they included in their private lives and used different relationships for different purposes.

One of the most important sites of association were taverns, in which many enslaved people spent time. Taverns were central communal gathering places in New England. Every rural community hosted at least one inn or tavern, and New Englanders—white, Indian, and black, free and enslaved—frequented them regularly. Not only were they spaces where people could have a drink and some food to eat but they also hosted entertainment in the form of live music and dancing, provided an opportunity to hear the latest news and gossip, and allowed people to play games and gamble.

Records abound about enslaved people patronizing New England taverns. Various colonial laws and local statutes criminalized for people of color certain features of tavern life, such as purchasing hard liquor or staying out late into the night. Nevertheless, enslaved people defied these laws. A Boston master learned about this defiance one night when he looked for his enslaved domestic who had not returned home for a few days. He decided to look for her in the neighboring town of Roxbury. After searching all day, it became late (after nine p.m., the appointed curfew time for slaves), when he heard noise from a local tavern and decided to enter. He opened the door only to be mortified. There, in the flesh, were a "Dozen black Gentry, He's and She's, in a Room in a very merry Humour, singing and dancing, having a violin." Helping the merrymaking was a "Store of Wine and Punch." The master hoped his encounter with such a disturbing scene, for a white observer at least, would convince other slave owners to prevent such "Nocturnal Frolicks."[14] Like the laws criminalizing black nightlife, however, these complaints did little to stop enslaved people from frequenting taverns.

And it seems that other tavern-goers welcomed enslaved people. They were not only paying customers, using the wages they earned on the farm or in the workshop, but many blacks were also musicians. They could provide entertainment for other patrons—and earn a little extra money for themselves. In June 1763, John Loveland, a local busybody, caught Quash, an enslaved man belonging to Wethersfield, Connecticut, farmer James Smith leaving a tavern after the "Negro curfew." Loveland stopped and apprehended Quash. He was going to take Quash before Elisha Williams, a justice of the peace, but before he could act, three men, Joseph Richard, Joseph Richard Jr., and Simeon Richards, intervened and with "Force of arms" assaulted Loveland. They beat the interloper mercilessly with "clubs staves & stones," allowing Quash to "escape from Justice."

Let us baldly state the facts of the case here: three white men intervened to protect an enslaved African man from being arrested and punished for breaking curfew. While the brief complaint filed by Loveland does not detail or speculate on what motivated the Richards to attack him, there are some clues. Other documents concerning Quash's life demonstrate he was a skilled fiddler. It seems, then, on the night of 22 June 1763, Quash provided that evening's entertainment at the local Wethersfield tavern. After performing, he took his leave. When Loveland stopped Quash outside the tavern, he infuriated the tavern's patrons, including the Richards. The three men intervened to shield an entertainer and fellow tavern-goer. Had Quash been arrested and prosecuted, it might have prevented him from fiddling in the future, depriving the community of a source of entertainment.[15]

Not all enslaved tavern-goers had the support of their communities like Quash, however. Often times, slaves patronized so-called disorderly houses. These establishments, illicit taverns operated by poor people out of their own homes, were magnets for enslaved people. Unlike many more reputable taverns, disorderly houses tended to welcome anyone willing to pay. They offered space for marginalized and maligned people to gather, relax, and talk among themselves. Such locations also, according to authorities at least, disturbed the peace. Loud and obnoxious, they created disorder. They also scared town officials, leading families, and middling people who saw them as places where conspiracies could be planned. For that reason, disorderly houses were often shut down quickly after opening. Nevertheless, in a game of colonial whack-a-mole, as soon as authorities shut down one, another popped up to replace it.

While enslaved people certainly gathered and associated in illicit spaces, they also attended and joined more legitimate colonial institutions, most importantly the many churches that dotted New England's landscape. During the earliest period of colonization, leading Puritans were ambivalent about converting slaves to Christianity. John Winthrop, the first governor of Massachusetts, described the Christianization of an enslaved woman he called "Dorcas the blackmore" in his diary. People like Dorcas, who eventually became a full church member, were rare in the seventeenth century.[16] Much of the ambivalence concerned questions about whether or not enslaved people had to be freed if they converted. Likewise, church membership was associated with civic freedoms, such as the franchise, and converting slaves opened the body politic to nonwhite people.

By the eighteenth century, colonial officials, religious leaders, and slave owners were comfortable with the idea of a Christian slave population. Leading intellectuals, such as Cotton Mather, found ways to justify conversion without freedom. Likewise, as New England's religious landscape diversified after the Glorious Revolution in 1688, other denominations, especially the Anglican Church, advocated the conversion and catechization of enslaved men and women. Timothy Cutler, the minister of Christ Church (Old North Church), an Anglican parish in Boston's North End, for example, used the pulpit to admonish his parishioners to baptize and convert the enslaved members of their households.

Enslaved people did not miss the message of Cutler and other leading New England divines. Almost every parish in the region, regardless of denomination, in rural and urban settings, and within congregations rich and poor, contained enslaved people, sometimes as full members and other times as attendees. The registers speak for themselves. Even in rural frontier New Hampshire, Reverend Timothy Walker of Concord recorded baptizing three enslaved people. In seaports, the results could be more spectacular. In the First Church of Salem, Massachusetts, records show that ministers baptized ten slaves between 1739 and 1758.[17]

The question remains why conversion became such a common phenomenon in the eighteenth century. Certainly, some enslavers believed

Christianity, especially its message of submission and obedience, could be a useful tool for controlling potentially troublesome bondsmen and -women. Other masters thought themselves to be good Christians and wanted to ensure everyone in their household received Christ's salvation as well. Nevertheless, it is important to view religion from the perspective of enslaved people too. While it is hard to discern the spiritual beliefs and practices of New England's slaves, church membership offered tangible benefits for slaves. All churches in New England were Protestant and emphasized the necessity that parishioners read the Bible. Thus, enslaved people often learned to read and sometimes even write. Likewise, church membership offered connections to the ministry, the church's community, and sometimes to powerful members of New England's ruling class. These connections could translate into help and access to material goods. Finally, being Christian meant enslaved men and women could lay claim to certain rights, privileges, and language that allowed them to communicate and appeal to authority and community.

Because of religious instruction, by the 1730s and 1740s, New England was home to a literate slave population with connections to the larger community and well-versed in religious doctrine. In short, being Christian gave enslaved people some, albeit not much, power. Much of this newfound power they exercised through religious practice, reference, and ritual. Phillis Wheatley, an enslaved poet and the first African American woman to be published, wrote using such strategies. Born in the Senegambia region of Africa and brought to Boston as a young girl, she had a relatively easy home life with her master and mistress, John and Susannah Wheatley. They saw to her Christian education, and by age twelve she was fluent in English, Latin, and Greek. Soon thereafter, she took to writing poetry. Wheatley was a brilliant poet, especially in her ability to deploy Christian language and tropes to lay claim to privileges and critique slavery. She often referred to herself and other people of African descent as "Ethiopian," for example. Any Christian reading her poetry would have instantly identified that reference, as Ethiopians appear in the Bible. In giving Africans a Christian past, she created empathy and community in the New England present.[18]

During the middle decades of the eighteenth century, the religious affiliation of enslaved people changed. In 1740, the evangelical revivalist

George Whitefield preached around New England. He offered a message of tolerance, peace, personal salvation, and spiritual equality. All of these appealed to the region's enslaved population, especially because Whitefield often specifically sought out and met with the black populations of various New England towns. The message of Whitefield and other evangelical preachers was attractive to African and Indian slaves, and they began to swell the ranks of the region's churches, both old and new. Timothy Cutler, a high Anglican priest, recorded baptizing thirty enslaved infants in the wake of Whitefield's revivals, while the new churches that broke off and emerged after the revivals offered communion and brotherhood to all who entered their doors.[19]

Perhaps no person better illustrates this latter trend than Sarah Osborn. A schoolteacher and wife of an impoverished sailor from Newport, Rhode Island, she saw an opportunity with the Whitefieldian revivals. She opened her own home for religious instruction and invited everyone in the community to attend. Eventually, her message of spiritual equality and individual salvation attracted a large and diverse audience, including many of Newport's slaves. Away from formal theology and religious learning, Osborn offered a more democratic and self-motivated version of religion, and this spirituality may have appealed to enslaved men and women looking to escape the rigors of everyday life.

Evangelical religion, however, was not the only communal escape for slaves. As in other facets of their lives, enslaved men and women engaged in public activities that could either involve whites or be racially exclusive. Slaves received permission to participate in a number of holidays and communal gatherings. Most popular were muster days, where town militias gathered to drill and conduct military exercises. These were monthly, all-day affairs that the entire community attended. Slaves, although prohibited from serving in the militia, nevertheless found ways to participate. They hawked food and beverages to attendees, played games of skill and chance, and marched and celebrated alongside the militia. Similar participation occurred on election days.

Not all public activities of enslaved people, however, revolved around the holidays of the white majority. Rather, slaves created their own public rituals. Funerals especially were important public occasions for New England's slaves. Combining West African, Afro-Caribbean, and

Euro-American practices, the funerals of black New Englanders were elaborate social affairs. Funerals could see hundreds of people—white, Indian, black, and of all social statuses—in attendance. Attendees often received gifts, were entertained by musicians, and could listen to bells ringing as the funeral procession wound its way through town streets. Over the course of the 1700s, the funerals of enslaved and free blacks came to be fairly remarkable. As funerals for whites became increasingly private, family affairs, those of blacks remained public spectacles. They were loud, boisterous, and disturbed the public peace. By the middle decades of the eighteenth century, many towns began limiting, if not outright banning, the large public funerals of black New Englanders. Boston, for example, passed an ordinance "for Preventing and Reforming Disorders at the Funerals of Negroes."[20] Such attitudes reflected concerns about large gatherings of enslaved and marginalized communities, an intolerance of behavior and cultural practices that were alternative to dominant norms, and fears of the possible motives of these ceremonies.

As authorities regulated black funerals, enslaved and free black New Englanders cultivated a distinctive regional tradition that garnered much attention from contemporary observers and subsequent historians. In that festivity, called Negro Election Day, enslaved and free Africans gathered in rural areas to elect a king or, after the American Revolution, a president. Drawing from West African ideas of kingship and mimicking white New Englander's election days, this festival allowed black New Englanders to congregate and select their own communal leaders. "Kings" and "presidents" were often leading members of the black community, recognized by both blacks and whites. The celebrations to elect these leaders could last close to a week and involved dancing, elaborate rituals, and plenty of feasting and drinking. Given the social isolation that many enslaved people in rural New England experienced, Negro Election Day offered a short respite from lives of drudgery and loneliness. It is not hard to imagine that these ceremonies were both spaces for socializing and places where people could find a partner and envision possibilities for mitigating some of the worst abuses of slavery.

Contrary to funerals, many masters and local grandees sponsored and endorsed Negro Election Days. They often gave donations and lent clothing. Much of this has to do with personal vanity, as masters, seeing their slaves as extensions of themselves, wanted their bondsmen and -women to be as lavishly dressed and pampered as their own social situation would allow. More cynically, most masters and local elites knew that no matter how dangerous allowing large numbers of enslaved and marginalized people to gather could be, it also acted as a pressure release valve. A week's vacation full of socializing might ensure better behavior or offer a privilege that could easily be stripped away for behaving poorly. Even the act of electing a king or president was a way for masters to trick slaves into believing they had some control over their own lives. Regardless of motive, in condoning Negro Election Day, masters and local officials allowed a black New England subculture and powerful notions of community to emerge.

Resistance

As enslaved New Englanders created families and fostered community, they also actively challenged the terms of their enslavement. Called "resistance" by historians, these acts took many forms and occurred in different spaces from the home to the workplace. Given the small-scale nature of slaveholding and low density of enslaved people in New England, resistance looked different there from other slave societies in the Americas. Although communal resistance occurred, most slaves engaged in individual acts to protect their time, bodies, and lives. Furthermore, the peculiar nature of New England society shaped how enslaved people engaged in acts of resistance and caused forms common to all slaveholding cultures, like running away, to look different in the region.

Before moving forward with what resistance to slavery looked like in New England, it is important to discuss what is and is not classified as resistance here. It is easy when studying slavery to fall into a "resistance trap," where every action by an enslaved person or group of enslaved people can be seen as a challenge to their status. When thinking about resistance, we have to center the experiences of the enslaved and not their masters. Did slaves truly believe they were fighting against their masters when they got married, participated in a funeral, or joined a church? Or did they have other motives? By making those acts about the relationship between masters and slaves, it strips enslaved people of their agency. It makes their actions wholly reactionary and deprives them of the ability to lay claim to certain privileges and opportunities.

With this understanding in mind, acts of resistance in New England tended to fall into two broad categories: individual and collective. The first and largest category, individual acts, were common throughout every slave society in the Americas. New England was no exception. There, enslaved men and women engaged in tactics to resist terrible working conditions, found ways to increase their autonomy, and extracted concessions from masters. Often called "weapons of the weak," these included slowing down work, feigning ignorance, pretending to be ill, pilfering items needed to subsist, and breaking tools. Slaves wielded all these weapons in New England.

One of the most common of these individual resistance strategies was running away. Endemic everywhere that slavery existed, absconding was even more common in early New England. Despite the small enslaved population in the region, two factors drove the actual act of running away and the belief, from the perspective of enslavers and colonial officials, that there was an epidemic of absconding. First, New England was the center of print culture in Britain's American colonies. By the 1740s, there were multiple newspapers published in the region's major towns. Boston alone had five newspapers in 1748. All these papers, looking for revenue, published runaway slave advertisements, and these advertisements are some of the most important sources for understanding enslaved people in New England. Masters, looking to recover their valuable property, had to be honest in these notices, offering an accurate physical description and including any identifying features. The proliferation of newspapers in eighteenth-century New England led to the creation of hundreds of runaway ads.

Second, enslaved men and women fled with great frequency. This was especially true for younger, single male slaves, who represented the majority of enslaved people in the region and the majority of runaways. New England's economy facilitated male slaves' absconding. In busy ports such as Boston and Newport, ship captains were always short-handed and desperate for sailors. Enslaved men hired on or stowed away. This practice became such a problem that runaway advertisements often warned "All Masters of Vessels" that aiding and abetting a runaway was a criminal offense.

Runaway slave advertisements are useful for the study of slavery in New England. They provide accurate descriptions of enslaved people and allow us to speculate on their circumstances more effectively than many other documents. The case of Pompey, an enslaved man belonging to Ichabod Goodwin of Berwick, Maine, proves instructive. Pompey was a habitual runaway, and Goodwin took out two advertisements, one in 1748 and the other in 1750, to recover his enslaved property. Both advertisements appear in the *Boston Post-Boy*, giving an idea how widely Boston newspapers circulated in the region. The first ad, dated 25 January 1748, offered a description of Pompey as a "thick-sett fellow." It noted the clothing he was wearing, including a "homespun double breasted light colour'd jacket" with pewter buttons, mentioned that one of Pompey's ears was "cut," suggesting that Goodwin may have cropped Pompey's ear—a common punishment for runaways but one that provided more incentive to abscond.[21]

In the second advertisement, from 23 July 1750, Goodwin offered more detail. Once again is the description of Pompey as a "short well-set Fellow," his cut ear, and his clothing, but now the reader learned that he spoke English well. Even more shocking, however, was Goodwin's mention that Pompey "had on a pair of Pot-hooks." This device, an iron collar with hooked iron rods sticking out, was for habitual runaway slaves. It prevented full mobility, especially in wooded areas. It is easy to imagine Goodwin, a blacksmith by training, exasperated with Pompey, crafting the pothooks to further torture and control his bondsman. But this time, Pompey was not alone. Another man, named William Najon, a "tall slim young Fellow" with a "light Complection," absconded with Pompey. Najon's status is unclear, but it seems he was some sort of servant. Goodwin must have believed the men were going to flee for the sea and not the interior because he issued a warning to sea captains not to "carry them off."[22]

Running away might have been one of the most common forms of individual resistance, but there were other, more violent forms of protest. It was not uncommon for enslaved people to violently assault

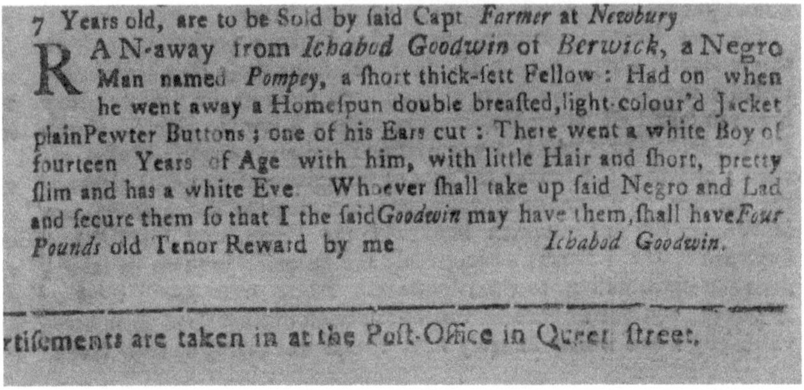

7 Years old, are to be Sold by said Capt *Farmer* at *Newbury*

R AN-away from *Ichabod Goodwin* of *Berwick*, a Negro Man named *Pompey*, a short thick-sett Fellow : Had on when he went away a Homespun double breasted, light-colour'd Jacket plainPewter Buttons ; one of his Ears cut : There went a white Boy of fourteen Years of Age with him, with little Hair and short, pretty slim and has a white Eye. Whoever shall take up said Negro and Lad and secure them so that I the said *Goodwin* may have them, shall have *Four Pounds* old Tenor Reward by me ⠀⠀⠀⠀⠀*Ichabod Goodwin*.

⠀⠀⠀⠀⠀⠀⠀rtisements are taken in at the Post-Office in Queen street,

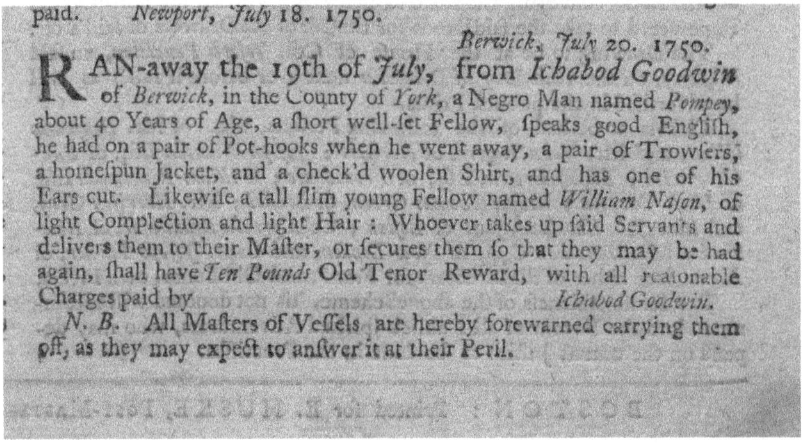

paid.⠀⠀⠀*Newport, July* 18. 1750.

⠀⠀⠀⠀⠀⠀⠀⠀⠀⠀⠀*Berwick, July* 20. 1750.

R AN-away the 19th of *July*, from *Ichabod Goodwin* of *Berwick*, in the County of *York*, a Negro Man named *Pompey*, about 40 Years of Age, a short well-set Fellow, speaks good English, he had on a pair of Pot-hooks when he went away, a pair of Trowsers, a homespun Jacket, and a check'd woolen Shirt, and has one of his Ears cut. Likewise a tall slim young Fellow named *William Nason*, of light Complection and light Hair : Whoever takes up said Servants and delivers them to their Master, or secures them so that they may be had again, shall have *Ten Pounds* Old Tenor Reward, with all reasonable Charges paid by ⠀⠀⠀⠀⠀⠀⠀⠀⠀*Ichabod Goodwin*.
⠀⠀*N. B.* All Masters of Vessels are hereby forewarned carrying them off, as they may expect to answer it at their Peril.

FIGURES 9 and 10. The runaway advertisements regarding Pompey, the enslaved man belonging to Ichabod Goodwin of Berwick, Maine. Collection of the Massachusetts Historical Society.

and sometimes murder their masters and mistresses or others who stood in their way. When Barney, an enslaved teenager in Middletown, Connecticut, castrated his master's son in 1743—most likely to spite his enslaver—the court did not know how to act. Violent retribution was deemed necessary, and the Connecticut legislature intervened, passing a special act to persecute Barney, citing the biblical injunction "an eye for an eye." Assemblymen sentenced Barney to be stoned at the gallows, repeatedly whipped, and finally castrated with red hot pinchers. Barney most likely perished from the torture.[23]

As the case of Barney shows, violent confrontation could lead to horrific consequences, and most enslaved people chose more subtle forms of violent protest. One of the most common was arson. New England newspapers and court records are littered with accounts of enslaved people burning property. It is often difficult to separate accidental fires—always lurking in a world illuminated by candles and heated by wood-fire—from deliberate ones. There are some clear cases of enslaved people committing arson in New England, however. In 1773, an enslaved boy in Connecticut torched his master's barn, killing ten horses and other livestock, because he was "tired of tending the creatures."[24]

Like arson, poisoning was another act of violent resistance that could avoid detection. Nevertheless, the records abound with enslaved poisoners, who sometimes poisoned masters, masters' families, and fellow bondspeople. Poison was especially destructive and hard to detect, thus it created deep-seated paranoia. There is a long history of enslaved people using poison in New England, but it reached a crescendo in the 1750s, when a rash of conspiracies using arsenic or, in eighteenth-century terms, "rats-bane" occurred. One of the first of these poisonings involved an enslaved teenage girl named Phillis. In 1751, when Phillis was around seventeen years old, she poisoned the children of her master, apothecary John Greenleaf. Given her master's occupation, it was easy to procure poison, especially as the enslaved girl came to loathe the task of caring for Greenleaf's three children. Phillis hoped to free up her time by killing the children and thought she could get away with poisoning them. The high infant mortality rate of the period would have made it seem little out of the ordinary for young children to perish. Ultimately, Greenleaf's two youngest children, John Jr. and Elizabeth, eleven months old and fifteen months old respectively, perished. Once suspected, authorities jailed and later executed Phillis.[25] To deal with the grief over the loss of two children, Greenleaf commissioned the young John Singleton Copley to paint portraits of them. Beneath Copley's cherubic images, however, lay the horrors of violent slave resistance.

In addition to violent and nonviolent individual acts of resistance, enslaved people banded together and with others to collectively resist

FIGURE 11. *John Greenleaf Jr.*, by John Singleton Copley, 1753–54. The child's cherubic aura and coddling of a lamb is meant to convey his innocence. John Singleton Copley, "John Greenleaf," 1753–54, 2002.611, Gift of Stuart and Rhoda Holzer, The Metropolitan Museum of Art, New York. Image copyright © The Metropolitan Museum of Art. Image source: Art Resource, NY.

their condition. Many of the strategies remained the same, however. Theft was also a group activity. In the middle of the night on 9 May 1752, William Healy, a white laborer, and Robin, a slave belonging to Cambridge, Massachusetts, merchant Henry Vassall, burgled the home of Vassall's neighbor William Brattle. With the help of Brattle's bondsman Dick, the two men stole a large chest containing hundreds of pounds sterling worth of paper currency. Joseph Luke, another poor white, was supposed to help the men abscond with the chest but was too drunk to assist. Rather, Healy and Robin decided to bury the chest in Vassall's yard. They then convinced another enslaved man in the Vassall household, Toney, a loyal footman, to take the paper currency into Boston in small amounts and convert it into coinage. Needless to say, the scheme fell apart and the conspirators faced prosecution. In their depositions to the court, the men explained the whole point of the robbery in the first place. They planned to use the coinage to purchase passage on a vessel to "go to Cape Breton and from thence to France."[26] Without doubt, the men knew that French law considered metropolitan France to be "free soil" where slavery was outlawed and could not exist. Thus, they concocted an elaborate currency pilfering to find their freedom.

Conspiracies involving theft and plans to escape are relatively common in the record. Less conspicuous are actual violent slave conspiracies, which sought to overthrow or unsettle the colonial order. Indeed, in the long history of New England slavery before the American Revolution, there is only one episode similar to the conspiracies to destroy slavery that occurred in other parts of the Americas. In 1723, a group of enslaved men allegedly planned to burn Boston to the ground. Of the seven arrested, there was only enough evidence to prosecute and execute one man, named Diego, the alleged ringleader. Compared to some of the massive conspiracies and rebellions in places like Jamaica, New York, and Louisiana, where hundreds were executed without due process, the Boston episode pales in comparison.[27]

The question, however, remains as to why massive slave conspiracies did not occur in New England. Part of it was demographic. In only two towns, Boston and Newport, did the enslaved population reach more than 10 percent of the total. Conspiracies were harder to plan and execute in areas where large numbers of enslaved people did not live in proximity to one another. In rural areas, some towns only had one or two slaves. Being so outnumbered meant that potential conspirators knew rebellion was outright suicide. Nevertheless, New York City, where slaves comprised about 25 percent of the population (the same as Newport), experienced two massive slave conspiracies in 1712 and 1741.

Since demographics do not offer a total explanation, other factors may have been at play. Unlike other parts of the Americas where rebellion was endemic, New England's slaves came from a variety of places in Africa and the Americas. Many slave rebellions were coordinated acts by individual ethnic groups like the 1760 Tacky's Revolt in Jamaica, which was largely executed by the Coromantee, Akan-speakers from West Africa. In New England, there was rarely a large concentration of individual ethnicities.

That said, there is some tantalizing evidence that suggests certain acts of resistance coincided with the influx of specific groups of slaves. In the 1730s and early 1740s, for example, Boston—like the other British North American colonies—witnessed an influx of "Spanish Negroes." During Britain's wars with Spain in the same time period, British American privateers captured and raided Spanish ships. As part of the plunder, they would seize sailors and other people of color, regardless of their legal status, and sell them as slaves. These men and women, many who were free subjects of the Spanish crown, vehemently and often violently resisted enslavement. Boston's newspapers are riddled with accounts of these "slaves" running away or challenging their enslavement. In one case, a group of six "Spanish Negroes" stole a boat—they were skilled mariners after all—and attempted to flee to Spanish Florida. The ship was ill-equipped for a long voyage, however, and the men were soon apprehended.[28]

Even more tantalizing—and circumstantial—is the possibility that the epidemic of poisoning by slaves in the 1750s can be linked to the influx of enslaved people from Dutch Suriname. The New England–Suriname trade grew rapidly in the 1740s and 1750s. Slaves were an important commodity exchanged between the two regions, to the point that towns like Boston, Newport, and New London had many resident slaves from Suriname. These people had experienced a different slavery than that in New England. Significantly, poisoning was ever-present in the Dutch colony, as slaves poisoned whites, each other, and free people of color. Indeed, one historian has found that 36 percent of all cases involving slaves in the colony's courts concerned poisoning.[29] Such a plurality demonstrates the omnipresence of poisoning in Surinamese slave society. It is not hard to imagine enslaved people from that colony, forcibly carried to New England, using poison for their own ends and teaching fellow slaves its effectiveness for challenging their enslavement.

These two cases aside, mass resistance to slavery was relatively rare in New England. Open rebellion would have been futile in the region where the white majority could quash any rebellion. Rather, most engaged in individual acts of resistance. They sought to challenge their status, protect their family and friends, improve their material life, and ameliorate their condition.

Enslaved men and women in New England created family, built communities, and resisted their enslavement. Families often looked different from those of New England's white majority, as slave spouses lived in separate households; couples did not always solemnize their marriages; and bondsmen sought free women, especially Indians, as mates to ensure freedom for their children. Nevertheless, these partnerships had standing in law and practice. Likewise, enslaved people associated with one another and other people in the community. They played games, drank, relaxed, and fornicated with the region's lower classes, and congregated in taverns and marginal spaces. They also joined the region's many churches, finding salvation and material benefits in association. Finally, enslaved people resisted their enslavement. While collective, violent action was rare, slaves nevertheless found ways to individually challenge their status, and many of these tools, such as running away, could be effective.

As slaves in New England formed families and friendships and found creative ways to challenge their slavery, by the early 1760s, they confronted new challenges and possibilities. No amount of collective resistance or community could prepare slaves for the upheaval caused by Britain's attempts to reform its colonies and those same colonies eventually declaring their independence and creating a new republic. While the world was turned upside down, it created space for enslaved New Englanders to radically alter their situation.

CHAPTER 6

REVOLUTION AND EMANCIPATION

FOR THE ENSLAVED people who lived in New England, the American Revolution upended their lives, presented new opportunities, and created fresh obstacles to finding full freedom. Indeed, the revolution is the most important event for understanding the end of slavery in New England. As rhetoric and new ideas about liberty and freedom spread across the region, real change could finally be achieved. For a brief moment, everything seemed possible, including the full-scale abolition of slavery.

Imperial Crisis

The decline of slavery in New England coincided with what historians call the Imperial Crisis (1763–75). It was a moment of widespread resistance to attempts at colonial reform and taxation from Britain. It was also a moment of transformation. It began with colonists' articulating their privileges as English subjects and ended with them making arguments about the universal rights of humankind and creating an independent republic. Ever attentive, enslaved people in New England latched on to these larger intellectual trends and protest movements. In many ways, however, the Imperial Crisis was also a moment for slaves to repurpose the unique characteristics of New England slavery—

namely relatively wide-scale literacy and access to information—into tools for achieving freedom and emancipation. They even crafted their own protest movements. Such activism captured the attention of white observers. Some of these people came to sympathize with the plight of slaves and argued for abolition, while others were scared by the potential chaos of black political activism.

Of the many intellectual changes that occurred during the Imperial Crisis, one of the most profound concerned the morality of slavery. Before the 1760s, there was little criticism of slavery as an institution. Regardless of its brutality and inhumanity, slavery was ultimately a pragmatic, commonplace solution to labor shortages. As early as 1764, during the first major protests against parliamentary authority, antislavery voices emerged. One of the most important figures in this conversation was James Otis, a lawyer, politician, and defender of colonial interests from a leading Massachusetts family. In his pamphlet *The Rights of the British Colonies Asserted and Proved*, Otis penned an important and original argument regarding slavery.

While discussing natural rights, Otis claimed that colonists "by the law of nature free born, as indeed all men are, white or black." All men, in Otis's estimation, had rights regardless of race. There was little justification to enslave another besides race. Otis worried about the consequences of slavery because it was "the most shocking violation of the law of nature," "diminish[ed] the idea of the inestimable value of liberty, and ma[de] every dealer in it a tyrant." Such actions had consequences, Otis declared, and it was "a clear truth, that those who every day barter away other mens liberty, will soon care little for their own."[1] In one short paragraph, James Otis undercut all the justifications for slavery and raised the dire prospects of those who insisted on its maintenance. Although Otis may have been something of a hypocrite on the issue—he grew up in a slaveholding family—for an elite man to make such an argument suggests changing attitudes toward enslavement and the potential unleashed by the Imperial Crisis.

As the crisis caused some to rethink the morality of slavery, abolitionist sentiment could be found outside the protests against parliamentary authority. One of the most important hotbeds for antislavery activity in New England was within evangelical and Quaker communities. Rhode Island, home to large populations of both, came to harbor many divinely inspired abolitionists. That their home colony was also the epicenter of the North American slave trade and entirely dependent on the fortunes of the West Indies was not lost on these activists. Rather, it sharpened their critiques and made them even more vocal and forceful in their appeals.

One of the most important figures in this movement was Reverend Samuel Hopkins. A Congregational minister, Hopkins became close friends with Sarah Osborn, the evangelical woman who allowed slaves into her home, after she helped secure him a position as pastor at Newport's First Church. Hopkins, who would later go on to edit and publish Osborn's memoirs, was enamored with her commitment to preaching to everyone. While many factors inspired Hopkins's anti-slavery sentiments, one of the most important was his encounter with the enslaved people attending Osborn's gatherings. Meeting with slaves caused an awakening in Hopkins and generated sympathy for their plight. Combining this feeling with his evangelical commit-ment to spiritual equality, Hopkins became a vocal critic of slavery, publishing and preaching on the subject and adamantly maintaining that "God hath made of one blood, all nations."[2] Hopkins was one of many evangelical and Quaker figures that came out against slavery in the 1760s and 1770s, inspiring congregants to accept the immorality of slavery.

Changing attitudes toward slavery also had the potential to cre-ate conflict in a region so economically entwined with the institution. The Brown brothers of Providence, Rhode Island, demonstrate how these debates threatened to tear at the very bedrock of New England society: the family. There were four Brown brothers, Moses, Joseph, Nicolas, and John. All four men were merchants involved in planta-tion provisioning and the slave trade, including jointly financing the voyage of the slave ship *Sally* in 1764. It was ultimately a failure, caus-ing Nicolas to demur from slave trading ever again and Moses to turn against the noxious trade entirely. Most famously, the brothers funded the construction of the College in the English Colony of Rhode Island and Providence Plantations, now Brown University, an institution, like many in New England, endowed from the proceeds of slavery.

During the Imperial Crisis, the Brown brothers began to drift apart. Moses converted to Quakerism, turning his back on the Baptist faith of his ancestors and brothers. In doing so, he also began to accept and articulate Quaker arguments in favor of abolition. He broke with his brother John, refused to invest in any additional slaving voyages, and freed all of his own slaves in 1773. By the time of the American War of Independence, Moses was an outspoken abolitionist and sponsored legislation to ban the slave trade and end slavery in Rhode Island. He went on to help enslaved people win their freedom, assist freedmen and -women legally and financially, and eventually became one of the founding members of the Providence Society for Abolishing the Slave Trade, a civic association that sought to abolish the slave trade not only in Rhode Island but across the United States. Meanwhile, Moses's brother John remained deeply committed to the slave trade, increasing his investment throughout the 1770s, 1780s, and 1790s. He was such an ardent slaver that in 1797, he was one of the first people prosecuted by the U.S. government for violating laws restricting the slave trade. And he publicly defended his stance on the trade, openly sparring with Moses in print over abolishing the slave trade. Although Moses's ideas regarding the morality of slavery eventually won out, the debates created a deep rift in the Brown family.

The ideas of men like Moses Brown, James Otis, and Samuel Hopkins were not merely debated in parlor and pulpit; they were also put into action. We can see this most clearly in the notary records of Ezekiel Price. Throughout his long career, Price recorded manumissions from masters freeing enslaved men and women. Most slave owners justified freedom by noting how loyal, faithful, or hardworking a slave was. In 1768, for example, Susannah Ellis of Hopkinton, Massachusetts, freed her "Trusty Negro Man" Charles.[3] Over time, ideas of natural rights and the immorality of slavery drifted into Price's notary books. In another manumission from 1779, eleven years later, Ralph and Elizabeth Inman of Boston freed their bondsman William "in Consideration of the Rights of Humanity And of the long and Faithful Services."[4] While the language of trust and hard work still appear in this manumission, the first reason the Inman's listed for freeing William were the "Rights of Humanity." Obviously, the Inmans, living in the midst of revolutionary upheaval and rebellion against alleged British tyranny, saw the contradictions of fighting for their own liberty while owning slaves.

Although it is clear that white attitudes toward slavery shifted during the Imperial Crisis, it is important to not overemphasize these changes. People like Moses Brown, Otis, Hopkins, and the Inmans were still in the minority in the 1760s and 1770s. Many white New Englanders remained on the fence regarding slavery or still favored it. Compounding this ambivalence was the fact that trade with the slave societies of the West Indies was central to the region's economy. Small farmers and great merchants alike depended on this trade, and criticism of slavery could undermine commercial connections.

Likewise, focusing on the attitudes of whites ignores the most important factor pushing abolition forward: black New Englanders. During the 1760s and 1770s, two important developments occurred regarding people of African descent in New England. First, the free black population grew dramatically. Second, and partially fostered by the first, black New Englanders created a black intellectual tradition that articulated powerful antislavery and pro-emancipation sentiments. In short, while white antislavery attitudes mattered, they cannot be decoupled from the actions and activism of black New Englanders.

One of the major changes that occurred during the Imperial Crisis was the significant growth of a free black population in New England. Although there had been free and emancipated Africans and Indians in the region since the time of settlement, that population remained small. Legal restrictions, such as those on manumission, limited it. Nevertheless, by the 1760s, many enslaved people had found ways to work around these restrictions and find their freedom. Some enslaved men, for example, married free Indian and African women, meaning their children would be free. The first generation of those children reached their majorities in the midst of the protests against British authority. Self-purchase also became a popular way of obtaining freedom. Since many enslaved men worked outside the home for wages, they could scrimp and save and eventually pay their masters their own value. A number later went on to purchase their families out of slavery as well. Finally, despite the laws requiring bonds to be paid to the colony for manumissions, there seems to have been a steady uptick in the number of people freed in the 1760s and 1770s, most likely due to changing sentiments regarding slavery. That said, the last two factors, self-purchase and manumission, might have been driven by the economic crisis in New England following the Seven Years' War. This recession hit urban communities and tradesmen especially hard. Considering many enslaved people lived with artisans and in New England's port towns, it may have been easier for enslavers to rid themselves of their bondsmen and -women than continue to support them.[5]

Regardless of how free blacks became free, many became active in their communities and the emerging antislavery movement. One such free black activist was Paul Cuffee, the son of Kofi Slocum, a free black man from southeastern Massachusetts. After obtaining his freedom, Slocum acquired hundreds of acres of land around Dartmouth, Massachusetts, and married Ruth Moses, a Wampanoag Indian. When Slocum died, he passed his land to his children, who took his first name as their last. Shortly after Kofi's death, Americans took up arms against Great Britain. Like so many free people of color of his generation, Paul Cuffee became active in politics, joining Dartmouth's black community to petition for enfranchisement and civil rights in 1780. He refused to pay taxes until his and his community's rights were recognized, which eventually landed him in jail for a brief period. After this, Cuffee became a lifelong advocate for the rights of people of color in New England. Cuffee also became a wealthy entrepreneur and ship captain, activities that allowed him to support his activism financially.

Free black activists like Cuffee drew many of their ideas from an emerging black intellectual tradition in New England. Enslaved people in New England were among the most, if not the most, literate slave population in the English-speaking world. This literacy stemmed namely from slave owners and preachers looking to Christianize bondsmen and -women and give enslaved people access to the written word. As a minority population in the region, slaves engaged whites of different social classes and backgrounds. Proximity to printed materials and New England's marketplace of ideas exposed enslaved people to the latest intellectual trends of the Imperial Crisis, such as Enlightenment thinking, abolitionism, and natural-rights discourse. Slaves and freed people in New England drew from all these ideas, their own pasts, and their local traditions to craft a unique intellectual movement. Most poignantly and unsurprisingly, this movement advocated an end to slavery, unconditional emancipation, and civil rights for people of color.

One of the most famous figures of this emergent intellectual movement was Phillis Wheatley. Wheatley is an important figure in the history of slavery in New England because of her educational opportunities, her household arrangements, and her religious convictions. Yet, we would not know of her had she not been one of the first African Americans to publish. While she initially published poems in Boston's newspapers, few New Englanders could believe that an African woman was capable of such prose. In 1772, Wheatley went before a tribunal of leading men, including John Hancock and Governor Thomas Hutchinson, to verify she was truly capable of writing poetry. It is easy to imagine the young Wheatley, probably in her late teens, scared as she approached such men of standing. Nevertheless, she passed her trial with flying colors, and all eighteen men on the panel, many of whom had deep political grievances with one another, agreed that Wheatley was indeed a true and gifted poet. After her tribunal, she traveled to London, found a patron, and in 1773 published *Poems on Various Subjects, Religious and Moral*. Shortly after publication and her return to Boston, the Wheatley family freed Phillis, and she joined the swelling ranks of free blacks in New England.

Much of Wheatley's writing dwells on religious topics, although often in service to other concerns. Take for example her famous (perhaps infamous) poem "On Being Brought from Africa to America." The first two lines, "Twas mercy brought me from my Pagan land, / Taught my benighted soul to understand," suggest that Wheatley believed it was a blessing she was enslaved and brought to America. Otherwise, she would not be Christian. The last two lines—"Remember, *Christians, Negroes,* black as *Cain,* / May be refin'd, and join th' angelic train"— suggest an ulterior motive.[6]

In this poem, Wheatley argues that as Christians, blacks are members of a greater community with all the rights and privileges of belong-

FIGURE 12. Woodcut image of Phillis Wheatley from the first edition of her book *Poems on Various Subjects, Religious and Moral* (London: Archibald Bell, 1773). Library of Congress, Rare Book and Special Collections Division.

ing. Given the extensive Christianization efforts aimed at people of African descent, especially in the generation before Wheatley published, it would be hard to find slaves and free blacks in New England who had not been exposed to some variant of Protestantism. In a sense, then, Wheatley conceded the point that Africans were heathens but not people of African descent in the Americas. They, through the actions of the enslavers themselves, were part of a larger Christendom. As Wheatley's poetry demonstrates, one of the cornerstones of the emerging black intellectual tradition in New England was that black people *belonged* there and were members of a larger body politic.

While Wheatley's critiques of slavery and racism were subtle and embedded in her poetry, other black activists were much more forward in their criticism of the status quo. It is in moments of collective action that we get a better sense of the intellectual underpinnings of advocacy. A series of petitions filed by enslaved and free blacks in Massachusetts between 1773 and 1777 demonstrate this fact. Three of the seven petitions in particular provide insight into the larger Imperial Crisis. The first, filed in January 1773 and submitted to the entire Massachusetts government by "many Slaves, living in the Town of Boston, and other Towns in the Province," asked the government to take the "unhappy State and Condition" of enslaved people "under your wise and just Consideration." The statement offered a powerful, emotional appeal to the legislature, emphasizing, "We have no Property. We have no Wives. No Children. We have no City. No Country." Enslaved people needed relief. Although put forth by many people, only one, "Felix," most likely free black activist Felix Holbrook, signed it.

Couched in religious language and assurances of loyalty and hard work, the January 1773 petition demonstrates how people of color understood the latest news. After reminding the legislature that God considered all people spiritually equal, the petitioners mentioned God "hath lately put it into the Hearts of Multitudes on both Sides of the Water, to bear our Burthens, some of whom are Men of great Note and Influence; who have pleaded our Cause with Arguments which we hope will have their weight with this Honorable Court."[7] The reference to arguments on "both Sides of the Water" concerns a 1772 court case in Britain, *Somerset v. Stewart*, where the chief justice, William

Murray, 1st Earl of Mansfield, declared slavery incompatible with the laws of England and banned the practice on English soil. Word of the *Somerset* case raced around the British Empire and received much attention in the press. Many slave-owning colonists feared the decision's implications outside metropolitan Britain. As this petition shows, news of the case likewise reached enslaved people, who had their own interpretation. For them, *Somerset* offered an end to their bondage.

The second petition, filed in April 1773, made a similar appeal and was drafted by a "Committee" for their "fellow slaves in this province." Peter Bestes, Sambo Freeman, Felix Holbrook, and Chester Joie, all free black men, signed the petition. This one, however, introduced two ideas that give us insight into the intellectual world of enslaved people. First, the petitioners chided the legislature, reminding them that even the "the Spaniards, who have not those sublime ideas of freedom that English men have, are conscious that they have no right to all the service of their fellow-men, we mean the Africans." The Spanish allowed their slaves "one day in a week to work for them-selve, to enable them to earn money to purchase the residue of their time, which they have a right to demand." Referencing the Spanish legal practice of *coartación*, where slaves had the right to purchase their freedom, the petitioners sought to shame and encourage the legislature at the same time. Surely, free-born lovers of liberty sitting in the legislature would not allow themselves to be one-upped by the absolutist Spanish. Likewise, Spanish practice provided a model for those same lovers of liberty to rid themselves of odious slavery.

As this rhetorical strategy denotes, the petitioners were strategic, understanding the use of shame but also drawing on a vast knowledge of enslavement across the Americas. It is easy to imagine enslaved people reading about *coartación* in the many books available on slave law or hearing about it from enslaved and free black sailors freshly returned from smuggling runs to Spanish America. Knowledge and rhetoric combined to make powerful appeals to authority.

Second, the April 1773 petition introduced another concept that enslaved and freed activists discussed during the 1760s and 1770s: colonization. Once the legislature abolished slavery, the authors claimed, the formerly enslaved would follow whatever laws the legislature passed to govern them, "until we leave the province, which we determine to do as soon as we can from our joynt labours procure money to transport ourselves to some part of the coast of Africa, where we propose a settlement."[8] White New Englanders feared emancipation in part because it raised questions about what would happen to formerly enslaved people. To circumvent these questions, these petitioners proposed removing themselves to Africa. Whether this was a rhetorical strategy meant to assuage the minds of concerned legislators or sincere is impossible to tell.

Advocating for colonization was a tactic borne out of desperation. Even after repeated petitioning, the legislature did not address these petitions. The assembly most likely had its hands full with more pressing issues, at least for white colonists, regarding the looming war for independence. This inaction led to a final petition in January 1777. Unlike the previous two, this one had a much more frustrated tone and made a clear and assertive appeal for freedom. Filed after the colonies had declared their independence from Great Britain, it opened with a powerful claim that the petitioners were "detained in a state of Slavery in the Bowels of a free and Christian Country." Echoing the Declaration of Independence, the petitioners declared they had "in common with all other Men, a natural and unalienable right to that freedom." After filing "Petition after Petition," however, they had received no redress and hoped they "may be restored to the enjoyment of that freedom which is the natural right of all Men."[9] This petition demonstrates a deep commitment to natural rights, especially the notion that enslaved people had their natural liberty stolen. Only the legislature, the representative of the people, could address the issue. Powerful rhetoric and intellectual insights aside, this petition, like the ones that came before, did little to advance the cause of freedom.

Indeed, it seems the upsurge of black activism actually created a backlash against enslaved people in New England. Whites understood that advocating for their own liberty from British tyranny might stir more radical convictions in the people they owned. As early as 1765, towns banned slaves from participating in public festivities protesting alleged tyranny. Even more telling, in the late 1760s and early 1770s, there was a demonstrable uptick in the number of alleged slave conspiracies. These were often linked to a certain nervousness New

Englanders had regarding their changing relationship with the mother country. In 1768, while British soldiers occupied Boston, a number of townspeople complained that army officers were attempting to recruit slaves to help them tyrannize the populace. Like most of these alleged conspiracies, this one came to naught. It was the consequence of a few drunken comments made by a soldier.

Other conspiracies, however, can be directly linked to black activism. In September 1774, Abigail Adams wrote to her husband, future president John Adams, while he was attending the First Continental Congress. She informed him that there had "been in Town a conspiracy of the Negroes." The details were unclear, but it seems an enslaved person revealed the plot to authorities after warning others against proceeding. According to this informant, the slaves found "an Irishman to draw up a petition" to General Thomas Gage, the military governor who occupied Massachusetts following the Boston Tea Party, and promised "they would fight for him provided he would arm them and engage to liberate them."[10]

Adams had few other details regarding the conspiracy, but her story can be linked to actual documents. In the same series of petitions slaves and free blacks sent to the Massachusetts government, two additional ones stand out. In May and June 1774, enslaved and free black activists sent petitions to General Gage. These are largely similar to the others with their emotional and rhetorical appeals and use of natural-rights language. The language is so similar, in fact, that it is doubtful that an "Irishman" wrote them. While there are some differences in these petitions meant to appeal to Gage, such as a reference to many enslaved people being Anglicans in the May 1774 petition, neither of them offered to help him fight the rebels. Rather, they appealed to him as governor of Massachusetts.[11]

And that was probably where black activists made their fatal error. Short of an additional petition pledging support to Gage between June and September 1774—a possibility—the real problem was recognizing Gage as a legitimate authority. By fall 1774, most white New Englanders saw Gage as an instrument of tyranny, sent to destroy colonial liberty. For blacks to acknowledge him as the rightful governor of Massachusetts, which he was, would have raised alarm bells for white colonists. Lurking in their homes may have been servants of parliament, crown, and tyranny. As Americans grew closer to open conflict with the mother country, black activism, even that which largely conformed to a decade of advocacy, came to be something openly feared.

War of Independence

From the moment that European Americans took up arms against the British in April 1775, enslaved and freed people were involved in the fight. Indeed, one of the first Americans wounded at the Battle of Lexington and Concord, the first engagement of the War of Independence, was Prince Estabrook, an enslaved man. Estabrook was the first of many black New Englanders to fight during the conflict. The war itself created opportunities for enslaved people to escape or otherwise challenge their status. While the war in New England had largely ended by 1777, black New Englanders disproportionally took up arms to fight for the new United States and Great Britain.

Ground zero for black New Englanders serving during the war was Rhode Island. The state had a sizable enslaved population that patriot leaders saw as potential military manpower. In February 1778, the Rhode Island General Assembly passed a law that allowed "every able-bodied negro, mulatto, or Indian man slave" to enlist in one of two battalions created for men of color. For pledging to fight, enrollees received their freedom. Rhode Island would in turn compensate masters whose slaves chose to enlist. By October, 74 men had enlisted, and treasury accounts note that the state paid for 110 slaves. These men mustered in the Rhode Island First, a mixed-race battalion consisting of emancipated slaves, free blacks, free Indians, and white officers.[12]

Although a segregated unit, the Rhode Island First was a combat battalion. Unlike most people of color serving in the war, who tended to be cooks, laundresses, and laborers, the men of the Rhode Island First fought. After mustering in 1778, the battalion remained in the field until 1783. The men saw action in New England, New York, New Jersey, and even fought at Yorktown, the battle that ended the war in North America. They came to be renowned for their bravery, as one observer described when facing veteran Hessian soldiers. "Three times in suc-

FIGURE 13. *Soldiers at the Siege of Yorktown,* by Jean-Baptiste Antoine DeVerger, water-color, 1781. The painting includes a black soldier from the Rhode Island First. Courtesy of Wikimedia Commons.

cession [the First was] attacked . . . by well disciplined and veteran troops," explained the witness, "and three times did they successfully repel . . . and thus preserved our Army from capture." Such tenacity earned the freedmen of the First a reputation as a reliable and integral combat unit. In exchange for that bravery, the formerly enslaved men were forever free.[13]

Many enslaved and free blacks served in the Continental Army. Under an agreement between the newly independent nation and the individual states, each state had to contribute a certain number of soldiers and funding to the army. States struggled to find the requisite number of soldiers, given that most white men were farmers and wished to serve close to farm and family. While the commander of the army, Virginia soldier and slave owner George Washington, was at first reticent to allow nonwhite soldiers to enlist, desperation for manpower and a fear that the British would recruit and arm enslaved people belonging to patriot rebels eventually won him over. In 1777, the Continental Congress allowed for the enlistment of black soldiers. These men would be integrated into other units and fight alongside white soldiers. The rewards for enlistment varied from state to state, but in New England, service often came with freedom.

While the vast majority of enslaved people lived in the southern states, most of the Continental Army's black recruits came from New England. According to the 1790 federal census, in Connecticut 20 percent of the black men listed as heads of households had served in the army, giving us a sense of the scale of military service among black males from the region.[14]

Pension records are one of the best sources for finding black soldiers from New England who served in the Continental Army. In 1818, the U.S. Congress passed an act granting pensions to all veterans of the Continental Army and their widows. Black veterans, usually labeled "colored" in the records, and their wives came forward and claimed these pensions. The act required witnesses to corroborate the stories told by pensioners. For that reason, these records are extraordinarily helpful for understanding who served, what they did while in uniform, and their fate following the cessation of conflict. For instance, Primus Jacobs was an enslaved man from Salem, Massachusetts, who fought in the Continental Army. After the passage of the Pension Act, his widow, Dinah, came forward to claim his pension. Testifying on Dinah's behalf was Benjamin Jacobs, the son of Primus's former master. Benjamin spoke glowingly of Primus's service, describing how he served between March 1776 and March 1778, fought at Saratoga, and survived the nightmarish winter at Valley Forge. Primus returned to Salem after winning his freedom through his enlistment and remained acquainted with the Jacobs family. Government officials, convinced by Benjamin's testimony, awarded Dinah a $520 pension—no small sum in 1818.[15]

Notably, many enslaved men used military service as purely an avenue for freedom. Commodore Samuel Tucker, an American naval officer, fired off an annoyed letter to a subordinate serving onboard the frigate *Boston* in January 1778. Tucker demanded the lieutenant find and "Apprehend . . . Two Negro Men who belong to the Ship" who had escaped.[16] The commodore believed that the men used their enlistment as an opportunity to abscond altogether.

There were also two sides in the conflict, and many enslaved New Englanders chose the British Empire over the fledgling United States.

Indeed, of the estimated twenty thousand enslaved people who took up arms during the conflict, 75 percent fought for the British. Most of these slaves, however, were from the southern states, where the British Army actively recruited among the enslaved population and welcomed runaways. Northern slaves tended to serve in the Continental Army and state militias. That said, some enslaved New Englanders did throw their lot in with the British. When the British Army departed New York at the cessation of conflict in 1783, they created a register, called the Book of Negroes, to document all the people of African descent who were leaving with the army and would be resettled. Of the nearly 3,000 entries, fewer than 150 were slaves from New England.[17]

Relatively small number aside, we can track the experiences of black New Englanders who sided with the British. One fascinating story is that of enslaved Bostonian Pompey Fleet, the son of Peter Fleet, the enslaved printer and engraver. Pompey was owned by Thomas Fleet Jr., the son of Peter's owner, and like their fathers, Pompey and Thomas Jr. were printers. Likewise, much of the defiance that Peter Fleet recorded in his imprints, Pompey inherited. He challenged and befuddled Thomas Jr. throughout their lives but saw a particular opportunity when he came into contact with the British Army.

Shortly after the arrival of General Thomas Gage and the first British troops to occupy Boston in May 1774, Pompey Fleet defied his master. In early June, Thomas Fleet Jr. published a runaway advertisement looking to recover Pompey, who had "Lately broke out of Bridewell," the town jail. Why Pompey was in jail is unknown, but masters would often request that the authorities jail incorrigible slaves. Thomas Jr. also made sure to note that he believed Pompey to "be lurking about with an Indian Wench, whom he calls his Wife."[18] Like many enslaved New Englanders of his generation, it seems Pompey cohabitated with an Indian woman.

It is unclear if Thomas Jr. ever found Pompey because the next time the enslaved man appears in the records, he was no slave at all. He was listed in the Book of Negroes in 1783 as free; having obtained his freedom, he had "left" his master during the "Evacuation of Boston." It seems Pompey escaped from Boston when the British Army evacuated in March 1776 and then resettled with them in New York City.

During the war, Pompey continued as a printer, working with a loyalist named Alexander Robertson to publish the *Royal American Gazette*.[19] When the army evacuated after the war, he traveled with his employer to Nova Scotia where he resettled for a few years and continued working as a pressman. Pompey's employer left Nova Scotia in 1786, but he remained until 1791 when he appeared in the records again. This time, he was on a list of emigrants to Sierra Leone, a colony in West Africa recently founded by the British to resettle black loyalists. Although the records are unclear, Pompey possibly became the first printer in Sierra Leone.[20] As we can see, military service and the opportunities for freedom created by the War of Independence could literally send black New Englanders across an ocean.

Emancipation

After the United States secured its independence in 1783, the new nation had to face the question of slavery. How could a nation dedicated to liberty and equality condone slavery? New Englanders had to confront this question with even greater concern. The region was the epicenter of revolutionary activity, and the hypocrisy of owning slaves even more glaring. Disproportionately, enslaved men from New England served in the military. By the 1770s, the region was a hotbed of antislavery activism and New Englanders of color vociferously demanded their rights. It should come as no surprise, then, that in the two decades following the Declaration of Independence, New Englanders, white and black alike, systematically destroyed slavery. The impulse for abolition came from above from the revolutionary governments and below from the enslaved themselves.

Even before the end of the war, the New England states began to formally dismantle slavery. The first to abolish slavery, however, was not one of the old colonial territories but rather a recently established polity, Vermont. Long a contested borderland between New Hampshire and New York, Vermont declared itself an independent republic in 1777. Although most people living there considered themselves Americans and desired to be part of the United States, Vermont remained independent until 1791. Mostly settled by white farmers from southern New

England, New Hampshire, and New York, and animated by the principles of the American Revolution, the new republic espoused especially radical beliefs. The constitution created shortly after independence extended the franchise to all men and supported universal public education. More significantly, Vermont banned adult slavery. Declaring that "all men are born equally free and independent," the Constitution of 1777 banned slavery and servitude after the age of twenty-one for men and eighteen for women.[21] While abolition only applied to adults, Vermont's government was the first to restrict slavery in the Western Hemisphere.

The older territories followed suit after independence. Legislatures in Rhode Island and Connecticut passed gradual emancipation laws in 1784. As the name implies, gradual emancipation meant that slavery was phased out slowly. In Connecticut, any children born after 1 March 1784 would be legally free but obligated to serve their mothers' masters until the age of twenty-five. Rhode Island stipulated the more common age of majority—eighteen for women and twenty-one for men. This status for these children, somewhere between slavery and freedom, was akin to indentured servitude or apprenticeship.

There was a logic behind this type of abolition, a combination of paternalism and pragmatism. Legislators knew they could not strip enslavers of their private property, especially in the aftermath of a revolution partially fought over property rights. The states could have compensated masters for slaves, but the former colonies were in poor financial shape following the war. Likewise, if the state purchased and immediately freed the slaves it had purchased, responsibility for any of the alleged problems of emancipation—poverty and criminality— could be blamed on the state. Finally, since the state would not free all slaves, legislators feared that free children born to enslaved women would have no real means of support.

Problems with these laws abounded. Slavery still existed for those enslaved before the passage of the laws. Few avenues to freedom existed already, and enslavers, seeing the writing on the wall, were less willing to part with their enslaved property. Likewise, the laws raised a number of questions. What, for example, would happen if a child born after the passage of the law had a child before the term of bondage expired?

Those "children" would have been sexually mature by the time their indenture ended and, especially in Connecticut, been thinking of starting a family. The status of their own children would be in jeopardy.

As the problems of these laws suggest, they were also the product of compromise. The negotiations involved help explain the highly conditional emancipation they offered. Connecticut, home to 6,464 slaves in 1774, the largest population in New England, is instructive. From 1776 until 1784, the state legislature, despite mounting pressure from activists and revolutionaries alike, only made small inroads toward abolishing slavery. Unlike Rhode Island, the Connecticut assembly voted down a law allowing enslaved people to enlist in 1777. About the only movement made from political institutions came in 1779, when the legislature approved a new manumission bill allowing masters to free healthy, able-bodied slaves without posting bond.

Emancipation, however, was an entirely different matter. In 1779 and 1780, the legislature voted against gradual emancipation bills similar to that later implemented. It took a hero of the American Revolution, Roger Sherman, a proponent of gradual emancipation, to finally enact a law. Even then, he and colleague Richard Law had to use a "back door" approach. They attached the emancipation provision (and one abolishing the slave trade) to a larger general law code that needed to be enacted. Historians still speculate as to whether or not all the legislators in Connecticut knew Sherman and Law had embedded gradual emancipation into the larger bill. Such jostling demonstrates that even in revolutionary New England, slavery was so embedded in the cultural fabric that it took celebrity and subterfuge to eradicate.[22]

After implementing gradual emancipation laws, states took aim at the slave trade. In no place was the slave trade more important than Rhode Island. In 1787, the Rhode Island assembly introduced an "Act to Prevent, and to Encourage the Abolition of Slavery and Slave Trade." While slave traders quickly rallied against the bill, it was to little effect. It helped that the war had ground the Rhode Island slave trade to a near halt, and even by the mid-1780s it was still not generating the profits of earlier times. Slave traders did not have the political clout they once had. Instead, other events intervened. As the title of the act implies, since slavery had already been "abolished" by the gradual emancipation act of 1784, the slave trade no longer made sense. Even further, slave trading—human trafficking—was often seen as the most odious part of the already noxious institution of slavery. It was, according to the law, "inconsistent with justice, and the principles of humanity." The majority of legislators agreed.[23]

Massachusetts, the most populous New England state, followed a different path to emancipation following the ratification of a new state constitution in 1780. In 1783, the chief justice of the Massachusetts Supreme Judicial Court declared slavery incompatible with the laws of the state. Called "judicial emancipation," the decision struck an immediate and devastating blow to the institution of slavery in the Bay State. That said, it was no less ambiguous and problematic than the gradual emancipation laws of Rhode Island and Connecticut. Understanding the origins of the 1783 court decision requires a thorough examination of the American Revolution in Massachusetts, the rise of abolitionism across the region, and the continued activism of enslaved and free black people.

Political change underpinned judicial emancipation. Black activists in New England began to formalize their fight for emancipation and civil rights in 1760s and 1770s. The most important figure in this movement was Prince Hall, a freedman. He had long argued for an end to slavery, signing the petitions to the Massachusetts government and advocating that Massachusetts allow blacks to serve in the army. Hall furthered this activism by creating institutions to support the fight against slavery. Most significantly, Hall sought to create space within the Freemasonry movement for people of African descent. Freemasons, a secret fraternity that emerged in the eighteenth century, advocated liberty and equality, making it attractive to men like Hall. While he could get little traction for recognition by white Freemasons in the colonies, he was able to convince British soldiers from Ireland to admit black members into their lodge in 1775. He began organizing blacks in Massachusetts into his lodge and received full rights from the Grand Lodge of England in 1784. African Lodge No. 1, as Hall's lodge was known, became a center of black activism and gave black men in Massachusetts a space from which to continue advocating for abolition and rights. The African Lodge was just one of many civic organizations created by New England's free blacks in the aftermath of the American Revolution.

Aiding this continued activism was the Massachusetts Constitution of 1780. Revolutionary principles, such as natural rights and republicanism, informed the document. John Adams, its author, also believed that slavery was antithetical to the spirit of American independence and placed nothing short of a "time bomb" aimed at destroying slavery into the constitution. Article 1, part 1—the very first article following the preamble—declares, "All men are born free and equal, and have certain natural, essential, and unalienable rights." No other article in the constitution limited rights based on race or status, meaning this section could be interpreted literally by anyone living in Massachusetts.

But why was this statement a time bomb aimed at slavery? Adams, a trained lawyer, was familiar with a legal technique used by enslaved people and their allies in New England. Called "freedom suits" by historians, these were court cases where enslaved people sued their masters for freedom. Freedom suits appear in court records as early as the late 1600s, but there was a dramatic uptick in them following the end of the Seven Years' War in 1763. Animated by the principle of imperial resistance, enslaved people, energized free black activists, and white lawyers began to file suit against masters.

Often, these cases were technically about being owed back wages. Since enslavers had frequently held enslaved people in bondage for years by the time slaves and their allies filed suits, the owners would technically owe hundreds of pounds sterling in wages—much more than the value of the slave. That left masters in a bind. If the court ruled on the side of the enslaved person, aided by some of the brightest legal minds in the region, the master would have to pay a substantial sum and acknowledge they had illegally held someone in captivity. They would be out hundreds of pounds and a valuable worker. That ultimately pressured masters to manumit before the case went to trial or have the court intervene and advocate for manumission alone. Nevertheless, results were mixed. Courts tended to rule in favor of enslavers unless enslaved people could make a compelling case. The Constitution of 1780 changed the dynamic. All an enslaved person would have to do is file suit and claim justice under article 1, part 1. And that was John

Adams's time bomb—a calculated measure deliberately placed front and center to undermine slavery.

It was two freedom suits that led to judicial emancipation in Massachusetts. The first was a case filed by an enslaved woman who would later go by the name Elizabeth Freeman. Known colloquially as "Bet" or "Mum Bet," Freeman was born in a Dutch-American community in New York. When her master's daughter married, she moved with the daughter to western Massachusetts. Freeman's mistress wed John Ashley, scion of a prominent family. As she grew up in the region, she proved herself willful, sharp, and forever at odds with her mistress. Freeman's sister also moved into the household, and one time when the sister made a small cake for herself, the mistress called her a thief. She heated a shovel in the fire and swung at the sister, but Bet intervened, her arm absorbing the blow. It cut to the bone and left a scar. Until it healed, Freeman left the cut exposed, and when people enquired, she told them to "ask missis."

It should not be surprising that such assertiveness eventually led Freeman to seek her own freedom. In 1780, she attended a gathering in her home town of Sheffield to hear the new constitution read aloud. Upon hearing article 1, she approached Theodore Sedgwick, a local attorney. Sedgwick harbored abolitionist sentiments and was probably moved by Freeman's declaration that she heard "all men are created equal, and that every man has a right to freedom. I'm not a dumb *critter;* won't the law give me my freedom?" Sedgwick accepted the case and also agreed to represent Brom, another slave in the Ashley household. When the Berkshire County Court of Common Pleas heard the case (*Brom and Bett v. Ashley*) in August 1781, the jury granted Brom and Bet their freedom. Soon thereafter, Bet took on the surname Freeman to advertise her new status. Most importantly, *Brom and Bett v. Ashley* established the precedent that slavery was incompatible with the Constitution of 1780.[24]

Nevertheless, Freeman's case was local. It was cited as a precedent two years later in the first freedom suit to appear before the Massachusetts Supreme Judicial Court. This case involved an enslaved man from Worcester County named Quock Walker. The case originated because Walker's master, James Cadwell, had promised to free him when he reached the age of twenty-five. Cadwell died when Walker was ten, and his widow married a man named Nathaniel Jennison. Jennison had no desire to honor Cadwell's pledge. When Walker was twenty-eight in 1781, he ran away and took refuge with Cadwell's brothers. Jennison retrieved Walker and beat him severely. That led Walker, with the help of the Cadwell brothers, to file three suits against Jennison, including a criminal assault case. These worked their way through local and appeals courts, eventually ending up before the Massachusetts Supreme Judicial Court in 1783 as *Commonwealth v. Jennison*. Massachusetts chief justice William Cushing presided over the case. He instructed the jury to consider the Constitution of 1780 and especially article 1. The jury agreed and granted Walker his freedom.

While historians once thought that *Commonwealth v. Jennison* was the end of slavery in Massachusetts, that is not true. Cushing's citation of article 1 was only in his instructions to the jury, and the case itself was not cited as precedent for ending slavery until 1807. Rather, Cushing said that the law did not uphold slavery in the state, making it legally indefensible. From 1783 on, all an enslaved person had to do was file a suit for freedom and they would obtain it. For those without the wherewithal or resources to go to court, simply absconding would work as well since masters no longer had a legal mechanism to recover their property.

As the cases of Quock Walker and Elizabeth Freeman demonstrate, the end of slavery in New England was largely brought about by the slaves themselves. Although aided by white abolitionists like Theodore Sedgwick, enslaved people often took the initiative and sought allies. Likewise, many acts challenging slavery did not involve whites at all. When asked how slavery in Massachusetts ended, Samuel Dexter, a local politician, placed it at the feet of the Constitution of 1780. But the document itself did very little according to Dexter. Rather, as soon as slaves heard article 1, they absconded "from the service of those who had been their owners."[25]

Dexter's observation was prescient and the attitudes he described seemed to spread beyond Massachusetts. By 1800, there were few enslaved people living in New England. Under the gradual emancipation laws in Connecticut and Rhode Island, there should have remained a sizable, if depleted, enslaved population. Census records demonstrate this trend. The first federal census in 1790 enumerated 948 slaves in Rhode Island and 2,764 in Connecticut. Those figures were already significantly lower than the number of slaves before the American Revolution. And yet, ten years later in 1800, 380 slaves lived in Rhode Island and 951 in Connecticut. In both places, the number of enslaved people declined by two-thirds between 1790 and 1800. This drop can be attributed to a number of factors, but one of the most important was the continued antislavery activism of enslaved and freed people in the region.

On 4 July 1788, a number of "black Inhabitants" of Providence, Rhode Island, gathered to celebrate the Fourth of July. This community, which had won its freedom during the American Revolution, engaged in a dangerous act. They were there in part to celebrate the ratification of the new federal Constitution. There was just one problem: Rhode Island had not yet ratified and was home to a large contingent of antifederalists (people opposed to the Constitution). Nevertheless, Providence's black community embraced the Constitution. They liked its provision ending the slave trade and believed it provided the order and structure to help undermine slavery across the nation and perhaps hemisphere. While there was much hyperbole at that Fourth of July celebration, blacks in Providence sided with the Constitution. They placed themselves under the new order and argued that it was ultimately an inclusive document that paid little regard to race. They, in short, were citizens.[26]

In many ways, the Fourth of July celebration by Providence's black community was the culmination of more than two decades of advocacy and antislavery activism. Since 1763, enslaved people and an ever-increasing number of free blacks began agitating for an end to slavery and an extension of civil rights in New England. These protests coincided with white colonists' own protests against British authority. When those colonists waged a war of independence against Great Britain, black New Englanders volunteered in droves and served the newborn nation—although a few also joined the British. Following the war, the New England states made moves toward formal emancipation, ending, albeit gradually and ambiguously, slavery once and for all. Central to this emancipatory moment was the continued activism of enslaved and freed people, who pushed whites, especially sympathetic ones, for abolition. And yet, even in this moment of triumph and while the struggle over slavery seemed to be ending, the struggle over emancipation was not. Indeed, it had just begun.

EPILOGUE

The Problems of Emancipation

ULTIMATELY, EMANCIPATION IN New England did not deliver on its promises of freedom, equality, and civil rights. And its legacies continue to haunt a region—and a nation—to this day.

It is important to think about the end of slavery in New England not as moment but as a process. While the most intense period lasted from 1760 to 1800, there were still people living as slaves or under the strictures of gradual emancipation in New England in 1865. They were only freed by the passage of the Thirteenth Amendment to the U.S. Constitution, which abolished slavery across the nation.

To fully understand slavery in the region, then, we must come to terms with emancipation, its meaning, and its consequences. Much like slavery more generally, emancipation demonstrated the entanglement of whites, blacks, and Indians in New England. What distinguished this period from earlier, however, is that abolition offered whites the possibility of *disentangling* themselves from slavery and, more significantly, from the people they used to own. Emancipation in New England is a story of whites' marginalizing, displacing, and segregating people of color all while distancing themselves from the institution of slavery. Thus, white New Englanders enjoyed the generational benefits of slavery while crafting a new society, one built on capitalism, industry, and free labor. Freed people, however, suffered from the generational trauma of slavery while being subjected to horrific racial bias and violence.

There were two larger changes that underpinned these problems of emancipation. First was the transformation of New England's economy in the late eighteenth and early nineteenth centuries. In short, the population of rural New England outgrew the productive capacity of the land and premodern farming techniques. Families were large, and New Englanders did not practice primogeniture—an inheritance practice where the oldest male heir receives a large percentage of the family's property. Rather, farmers divided land between their heirs, creating ever-smaller family farms that had to produce for an ever-larger population. This overtaxed the land, which began to give out. Farmers switched to more intensive animal husbandry, which helped their pocketbooks but not the food supply. Many poorer small farmers had nothing to give their children. As these children came of age, they found themselves in dire economic straits. They moved west and north to the frontier to start new farms or to towns in search of wages. The latter, called the "strolling poor," created a surplus of free, white labor for the first time in New England's history. The collapse of the rural economy solved the labor problem that had previously driven the expansion of slavery in the region. This fundamental transformation of the economy coincided with abolition, meaning freed people would enter an economy in crisis and a crowded job market.

Second, in the years surrounding the American Revolution, a virulent racism drifted into public discourse and society. While New Englanders had always held pejorative notions about people of African descent, it was in the decades before and after the Revolution that these ideas merged with "modern" science. Put another way, those ideas of African inferiority were no longer upheld by conventional wisdom but married to scientific "fact." Black people were no longer inferior because they lived in Africa, were not Christian, and were allegedly uncivilized. All those factors could be addressed and corrected. Rather, black people were inferior because of biology. Their incivility did not come from a lack of exposure to Western civilization and Christianity but from the idea they were too innately barbarous to comprehend Western civilization and Christianity. This new, scientific order, based on "objective" observation, demonstrated that black people were inferior. In short, while people of color faced discrimination and prejudice

FIGURE 14. *Dreadful Riot on Negro Hill!* (Boston, 1827). In the years following the end of slavery in New England, a virulent racism crept into public discourse. This satirical broadside depicts poor whites rioting and attacking freed people in their own community, demonstrating how the region's print culture helped to spread racist images and negative stereotypes about black people. Library of Congress, Prints & Photographs Division.

based off of their skin color before the American Revolution, white society became significantly more racist in the era of emancipation.

Although some white activists and people of African descent protested loudly against this new "scientific" consensus, these ideas permeated the American republic. Racism, in short, provided an easy answer to charges of hypocrisy. How could a new nation dedicated to liberty hold slaves? Because those slaves were African and too barbarous to take care of themselves, let alone be citizens. At least under slavery, whites provided food and shelter for benighted blacks. And what about freed people? Their economic, social, and political marginalization was not due to structural factors or the legacy of enslavement but rather because they were not white.

In regions where slavery was ending such as New England, the presence of free people of color raised serious concerns. Whites worried about how to build a functional republic composed of virtuous citizens in the presence of barbarous Africans. This mindset alone demonstrates an unwillingness to accept blacks as equals and the need to distance the nation from them. In New England, these attitudes drove the implementation of racist laws restricting and segregating black people in public. Many of these were based on acts governing slavery, such as banning blacks from purchasing liquor, serving in the militia, and voting. Others were new, such as the creation of segregated schools. Some whites recommended more radical measures such as colonization, where free people of color would be resettled on the frontier, in Africa, or the West Indies. Later, in the early nineteenth century, the region hosted some of the largest local meetings of the American Colonization Society, the primary organization that advocated sending black people abroad. Leading New England merchants and industrialists sponsored these meetings. Over time, many exasperated antislavery and civil rights activists, such as Paul Cuffee, came to accept colonization as the best possible option for black people to escape racism and enjoy their freedom. Others, however, insisted that African Americans should remain and lay claim to a country that also belonged to them.

The combination of economic change and racism further hurt prospects for black New Englanders. One of the most poignant examples of this fact is an observation made by John Adams in 1795. When asked why slavery ended in Massachusetts, Adams explained abolition occurred because of the "multiplication of labouring white people." "Common people," Adams described, "would not suffer the labour, by which alone they could obtain a subsistence, to be done by slaves." These "common people," rural farm children who went to cities looking for work, did not want to compete with enslaved or free black laborers. Adams went on to contend that had slavery not ended, "the common white people would have put the negroes to death, and their masters, too, perhaps."[1]

As always, Adams was an astute observer. As poor white men and women poured into New England's towns looking for work, they argued that employment was a fundamental right. But this right was racialized, belonging only to "common white people" and not to enslaved and freed blacks. Thus, while master artisans, merchants, and later factory owners really did not care who did the work as long as workers were capable and competent, poorer whites actively drove people of African descent out of the labor market and, if Adams is to be trusted, used veiled and sometimes open threats of violence to achieve that end.

Much of the marginalization and displacement of people of color can be framed around economic transformation and racism. Most insidiously, many masters sought to sell their slaves out of New England before they would be freed. Enslaved people were valuable property, and given that slavery was still legal everywhere in the Americas except the northern American states in the 1770s and 1780s, enslavers could always find a buyer. New England's slaves were also especially valuable. Many were skilled and had experience working trades in urban, maritime places. Furthermore, New England merchants were well-connected and could easily match sellers to potential customers.

It should come as no surprise that many enslaved people from New England were sold to Canada, especially Nova Scotia and New Brunswick. Settlers there were originally from New England and still had close commercial relations. Atlantic Canada's emerging regional economy, short of labor and oriented toward maritime activities, mirrored that of New England, making it a logical destination.

The West Indies, especially the non-Anglophone colonies, also featured as an important destination. Buyers there had few moral scruples over slavery and happily accepted additional enslaved laborers. One of the most compelling pieces of evidence we have for selling out concerns Massachusetts's then-governor John Hancock's attempt to stop the sale of three black men who had been kidnapped in 1788 by a ship captain headed for the French island of Martinique. Prompted by a petition signed by Prince Hall, Hancock and the French consul in Boston "wrote letters to the governors of all the islands in the West Indies," asking them to prevent the sale of the men and repatriate them to Massachusetts. Eventually, the men turned up on St. Bartholomew in the Danish West Indies. By that time, word had spread across the Caribbean, and the governor of the island prevented the men's sale. They eventually returned to Boston.[2]

Exhilarating story of John Hancock aside, there is quite a bit of evidence of a robust traffic in enslaved people, freed blacks, and indentured servants of color out of New England. Rhode Island explicitly banned the practice of selling people out in 1779, while Massachusetts followed suit in 1788. When Rhode Islanders formed the Providence Abolition Society in the 1780s, one of its primary tasks became preventing trafficking and finding freed people and slaves illegally kidnapped and sold out of New England. The group had a robust network of correspondence. Peter Thacher, a Massachusetts minister, wrote society leader Moses Brown to explain how he knew of "many instances of the negroes being kidnapped & privately conveyed away to Canada where they were sold for slaves." Meanwhile, Connecticut resident Jonathan Edwards Jr. wrote to Brown to explain he knew a man "employed in purchasing Negroes for exportation."[3] The laws prohibiting the practice and the Providence Abolitionist Society's activities suggest that selling out was extensive enough to cause alarm.

The work of Moses Brown and the Abolitionist Society also provides evidence of the experiences of kidnapped individuals. Some of these cases were nefarious, such as that of an enslaved boy named John Richman. In a 1793 letter to Brown, Philip Slead of Somerset, Massachusetts, explained that Richman "was Bornd in my house," most likely the child of an enslaved woman living in Slead's household. Slead then "Bound him" as an indentured servant until the age of twenty-one to a Silvester Richman. Silvester's relationship to John is unclear, although the Richman family was one of the largest slaveholders in southeastern Massachusetts before emancipation. John could have been the descendent of one of the Richman family slaves. Nevertheless, when Silvester acquired John as a servant, he "Clandestantly" sold him to "Cape Francois" in Saint-Domingue. Somehow, Slead learned that the boy did not make it to the French colony but ended up in jail on New Providence Island in the Bahamas. Slead begged Brown to "Take Som Methard to Releve" John by appealing to the "Govener of That Island or Som other way."[4]

As the case of John Richman and Slead demonstrate, kidnapping and selling out had a disruptive effect on the lives of people of color in New England. Selling out, for example, hurt the ability of freed black people to work and earn wages. In a petition asking the Massachusetts legislature to recover freed blacks illegally sold, Prince Hall described how "maney" free black sailors "who are good seamen are oblidge to stay at home thru fear" and could not be gainfully employed.[5] Others feared taking to the roads.

Paranoia featured prominently as well. In February 1789, notary Ezekiel Price copied the manumission certificate of one Charlestown, surname unknown. Charlestown had received the certificate in May 1777, almost twelve years earlier.[6] It seems that Charlestown went to Price to ensure that there was a copy on file, and he used Price's standing in the community to prove his own. In a world where unscrupulous whites kidnapped and illegally sold free blacks, who could blame him?

Even without the omnipresent fear of kidnapping, life could be unpleasant. Employment was often hard to come by, status and property rights were in no way secure, and most white neighbors were hostile. Consider the experience of Cato Freeman, a free black man from Cambridge, Massachusetts. As a slave, Freeman, then known as Cato Stedman, worked in his master's household. During the Battle of Bunker Hill, his master freed him. Cato, celebrating his newfound liberty, took on the surname Freeman. He then joined the Continental Army and served the entire duration of the war, despite being court-martialed during his winter at Valley Forge. After the war, he settled in Providence, Rhode Island, where he married a local free black woman and started a family. Life was not easy for the growing Freeman household. Cato had problems finding permanent employment and worked odd jobs around town like so many poor whites flooding into the region's urban areas.

Fearing Freeman would fall into poverty, the town selectmen of Providence ordered him and his family back to Cambridge in 1787. Instead of returning, the family moved to neighboring Cranston, Rhode Island. There, they once again came to the attention of town officials, but Freeman secured a letter from the selectmen of Cambridge that if the family fell on hard times, they would pay for Freeman's upkeep (most likely because they did not want another impoverished person returning to Cambridge). Letter in hand, the Freemans returned to Providence and even appeared on the 1790 census there. Nevertheless, in that same year, they once again came to the attention of Providence officials who this time forced him to return to Cambridge for good. Returning to the place where he had been enslaved on the public dole and in a renewed dependency must have been a humiliating experience. What happened to the Freemans after the order to return to Cambridge is unknown.[7] Uprooted and hounded by local officials, freed blacks like the Freemans joined thousands of strolling poor roaming New England in search of work and hope.

Those who fared best under freedom had access to property. Paul Cuffee inherited a considerable amount of land and capital from his father. He became a prominent ship captain and merchant. Venture Smith slowly purchased land and eventually established himself on a sizable farm. Another freedman named Caesar Marion lived in Boston and received his freedom in 1770, following his master's death. Among other occupations, Marion's master owned a blacksmithing shop so in addition to his freedom, Marion received all the "Working Tools belonging to the Blacksmiths Business" and six pounds sterling in cash.[8] It should be no surprise that he went on to become a prominent and prosperous blacksmith.

Even property was no guarantee of success, however. Indeed, racism often trumped property rights. James Davis was a freedman who lived in Charlestown, Rhode Island. His former master, Jedediah Davis, gave James his freedom and bequeathed him two-thirds of a working farm on his death. James apparently enjoyed this farm for a number of years until the early 1790s, when Jedediah's grandson Jedediah Browning had other ideas. Browning petitioned the Rhode Island General Assembly to declare that James Davis was unfit to manage his own affairs and needed to be placed under a guardianship "for the good of said negroman." Davis protested that such circumstances would "put [him] in slavery again," but to no avail. The legislature granted Browning's petition and stripped Davis of his land.[9] Despite the rank hypocrisy of propertied freeman of the legislature stripping another propertied freeman of his rights, it should come as no surprise. It was racist logic at work. Davis, a black man, could not manage property that he was given and thus a white member of the community had to intervene on his behalf.

All these problems were exacerbated by ambiguous emancipation laws. The judicial and gradual approaches to emancipation in New England created gaps and loopholes that could be exploited by slave owners, kidnappers, and government officials. This problem was most clear in Massachusetts. The 1783 decision *Commonwealth v. Jennison* did not abolish slavery. Rather, it stipulated that slavery was contrary to the Massachusetts constitution and had no standing in law. Worded in such a way, judicial emancipation placed the onus of ending enslavement on the slaves themselves. If an enslaved person could not access the courts or run away, such as vulnerable children and the elderly, they remained effectively enslaved. Often owners would refer to the enslaved people living in their households as indentured servants, a category that was still legal. Although the 1790 U.S. Census did not enumerate any slaves for Massachusetts, evidence suggests that most enslavers just listed their slaves as servants or census takers did not bother to record them. This use of legal loopholes and subterfuge meant slavery lingered in Massachusetts until the mid-1790s if not later.

Even radical Vermont, which had banned slavery in its 1777 constitution, still had slaves until at least 1810. The state had to pass an anti-kidnapping bill in 1786 preventing the "Sale and Transportation of Negroes and Molattoes Out of This State." In doing so, the legislature tacitly acknowledged that slavery still existed, describing how "owners of Negroes in this commonwealth" sold enslaved people out of the state despite "their being liberated by the Constitution."[10] Runaway slave advertisements appear in Vermont's newspapers as late as 1795, although mostly for enslaved people in neighboring New York, demonstrating the state was still invested in the practice. The legislature had to once again revisit the issue of kidnapping and passed a second bill in 1806, suggesting there continued to be enslaved people trafficked in and out of Vermont. Finally, in the 1810 U.S. Census, two men from Vermont claimed they owned slaves. While the number of slaves in Vermont was never large and certainly dwindled between 1777 and 1810, the persistence of slavery on New England's far northwestern frontier shows just how tenaciously enslavers clung to their human property and how engrained the institution was in the fabric of society.

Given the racism, fears of kidnapping, lack of economic opportunities, and ambiguous laws surrounding emancipation, it should come as no surprise that many freed people left altogether. Some freedmen that joined the army did not go back. Others moved to New England's most northern reaches, the Mid-Atlantic states, or the Trans-Appalachian

West. Combined with the large-scale selling out of enslaved people, voluntary movement out of New England created a diaspora of freed and enslaved people from the region. By 1800, they could be found in New York, Pennsylvania, the Northwest Territory, the southern states, Atlantic Canada, Britain, Sierra Leone, and the West Indies.

As blacks left the region or struggled to eke out a living, New England's white population never faced consequences for the sins of slavery. Rather, they enjoyed all the benefits of generations of slave ownership with little regard for those who suffered under its yoke. Even sympathetic whites or enslavers who realized the errors of their ways benefited. As we have seen, poorer whites, many who had never owned slaves, embraced racism and the marginalization of people of color. Not only did that lessen competition in the job market but it gave poor whites the psychological satisfaction of racial superiority.

Wealthier whites, especially those who owned enslaved people and invested in slavery across the hemisphere, enjoyed generational wealth built on the backs of slaves. No one personifies this phenomenon more than Rowland Hazard. A scion of the leading Hazard family of Rhode Island, he opened Peace Dale Manufacturing in South Kingstown in 1800. Four years later, he successfully mechanized the process for carding wool and other fibers to make cloth and soon became a leading manufacturer of textiles in early America. Hazard's success, however, was not foreordained. Before opening Peace Dale, he traveled the United States, failing in a number of business ventures before returning home to Rhode Island. The shocking part of Hazard's story is not that he eventually succeeded but that he had any money to open Peace Dale at all. As a failed businessman turned industrial magnate, Hazard found success both because of his innovations and because he had enough capital to continually experiment.

The source of this wealth was not hard work but rather family connections. Hazard's grandfather was Robert Hazard, who we met in chapter 4 and owned at least forty slaves, twelve thousand acres of land, and an extensive dairy, beef, and livestock export business. The slave economy created, fostered, and sustained by Robert Hazard generated enough capital for his grandson Rowland to become a leading American industrialist.

While enjoying the benefits of slavery, white New Englanders distanced themselves from the practice. Rowland Hazard once again proves instructive. His father was Thomas "College Tom" Hazard, a Quaker abolitionist who freed most of the slaves he inherited from Robert Hazard. Such an act of beneficence allowed Rowland to wash his hands of slavery and not concern himself with the plight of the freed people.

Rowland Hazard's attitudes reflected the feelings of the entire region. As slavery dwindled in New England, many whites, including those who owned slaves, began to define themselves as fundamentally different from other Americans, especially those in the South. New England was "free soil," so rich in liberty that slavery could never take deep root. Slavery, this line of thought went, was never important to the New England economy, was only practiced by a few wealthy families, and was a largely benevolent institution. Most importantly, white New Englanders realized the errors of their ways during the American Revolution and abolished slavery forever.

In crafting this narrative of a free New England, whites absolved themselves of the sins of slavery. Such a belief system allowed for whites to shift the blame for black poverty and immiseration away from the legacies of slavery and onto individual moral failings. Under this logic, if people could not thrive in a land of liberty and opportunity, they had no one to blame but themselves. White New Englanders, in short, made slavery—and its legacies—history.

In the face of these post-emancipation problems, freed people in New England persisted. Activism and institution-building continued, as did appeals and protests. And it took decades, but over time, change came. Black New Englanders became central figures in the struggle against slavery in the United States, keeping abolitionism alive and serving as inspiration to whites. They remained adamant in demanding rights and equality closer to home as well. By the time of the American Civil War, many of the racist and segregationist laws in the region, such as separate public schools, had been repealed. Nevertheless, racism persisted and still persists. In ways large and small, however, advocacy against those ideas and practices also persists.

Further Reading

Black Lives, White Worlds is deeply indebted to the many scholars, journalists, and popular nonfiction authors who have written on the topic of New England slavery. This section highlights many of those works though confines itself to books written on the topic. The study of slavery in the region has enjoyed something of a renaissance in recent years. Nevertheless, the standard, comprehensive work on the subject is Lorenzo Johnston Greene's *The Negro in Colonial New England* (1942). Greene's work, now nearly eighty years old, still remains the starting point for any study on slavery in the region. Greene combed the archives and published records from New England, and meticulously documented, organized, and interpreted the material he found. Most importantly, he is the first person to argue that slavery was vital to the economy of early New England. While the book is dated in places, it is still the foundational work for anyone looking for more information on the topic.

New England slavery is also the part of two classic works on the history of American slavery. The first, Edgar McManus's short and readable *Black Bondage in the North* (1973), provides a short, succinct legal and institutional overview of slavery in the region. For a more social and cultural approach to the topic of slavery in the United States, see Ira Berlin's *Many Thousands Gone: The First Two Centuries of Slavery in North America* (1997).

More recently, a number of books on New England slavery have come out for a popular audience. In *Complicity: How the North Promoted, Prolonged, and Profited from Slavery* (2005), three journalists from the *Hartford Courant* explore the relationship between early New England and slavery across the Americas, documenting the region's slaveholding practices and participation in the slave and provisioning trades. C. S. Manegold's *Ten Hills Farm: The Forgotten History of Slavery in the North* (2010) examines the Winthrop and Royall family estate in what is today Medford, Massachusetts, using it as a lens to understand slavery in the region. Allegra di Bonaventura's *For Adam's Sake: A Family Saga in Colonial New England* (2014) concerns the relationship among Joshua Hempstead, his enslaved man Adam, and their New London, Connecticut, community. Finally, Wendy Warren's *New England Bound: Slavery and Colonization in Early America* (2016) analyzes the earliest decades of slavery in New England and its relationship to English settlement and Indian displacement.

Beyond the popular histories, there are more specialized scholarly studies of slavery in New England. Some of these relate to individual places within the region. Rhode Island has perhaps the largest number of individual studies. Christy Clark-Pujara's *Dark Work: The Business of Slavery in Rhode Island* (2016) provides an overview of slavery and emancipation in Rhode Island from the time of settlement until the American Civil War. It is especially important because the author frames the book around the "business of slavery." The colony's entire early economy focused on providing commodities, including food and slaves, for slave societies in the Americas. For the classic study on Rhode Island's involvement in the slave trade, see Jay Coughtry's *The Notorious Triangle: Rhode Island and the African Slave Trade, 1700–1807* (1981). Other books explore individual regions and towns, such as Robert K. Fitts's *Inventing New England's Slave Paradise: Master/Slave Relations in Eighteenth Century Narragansett, Rhode Island* (1998) and Marjory Gomez O'Toole's *If Jane Should Want to Be Sold: Stories of Enslavement, Indenture, and Freedom in Little Compton, Rhode Island* (2016).

Beyond Rhode Island, other parts of New England have received attention. My *Unfreedom: Slavery and Dependence in Eighteenth-Century Boston* (2016) examines slavery in New England's "capital" and largest port town. Surprisingly, there is little for the rest of eastern Massachusetts, although some works not explicitly about slavery, such as Daniel Vickers's *Farmers and Fishermen: Two Centuries of Work in Essex County, Massachusetts, 1630–1850* (1992) and Gloria L. Main's

Peoples of a Spacious Land: Families and Cultures in Colonial New England (2001), do discuss the topic. For western Massachusetts, see Robert H. Romer's *Slavery in the Connecticut River Valley of Massachusetts* (2009). New Hampshire is the subject of Mark J. Sammons and Valerie Cunningham's *Black Portsmouth: Three Centuries of African-American Heritage* (2004), while information on Maine (then part of Massachusetts) can be found in Patricia Q. Wall's *Lives of Consequence: Blacks in Early Kittery and Berwick in the Massachusetts Province of Maine* (2017). A pioneering study of slavery in Vermont is Harvey Amani Whitfield's *The Problem of Slavery in Early Vermont* (2014).

Other studies of New England slavery take a more thematic approach. Like this book, these works tend to use examples drawn from the entire region. For a discussion of the emergence of slavery in the English-speaking world, which includes New England, see Michael Guasco's *Slaves and Englishmen: Human Bondage in the Early Modern Atlantic World* (2014). The enslavement of New England Indians is the subject of Margaret Newell's *Brethren by Nature: New England Indians, Colonists, and the Origins of American Slavery* (2015). Exploring the relationship among religion, race, and slavery is Richard A. Bailey's *Race and Redemption in Puritan New England* (2011). While Bailey focuses on the role of religion in creating race, John Sweet explores how enslaved and freed people attempted to incorporate themselves into white society in *Bodies Politic: Negotiating Race in the American North, 1730–1830* (2006). Other works have focused on black life in colonial New England. William D. Piersen's *Black Yankees: The Development of an Afro-American Subculture in Eighteenth-Century New England* (1988) explores the emergence of black folk culture, especially communal events like Negro Election Day. Enslaved and free black women are the subject of Catherine Adams and Elizabeth H. Pleck's *Love of Freedom: Black Women in Colonial and Revolutionary New England* (2010).

In addition to thematic and geographic studies, there are a number of biographies about enslaved and free black New Englanders. Venture Smith is the subject of a popular biography, Chandler B. Saint and George A. Krimsky's *Making Freedom: The Extraordinary Life of Venture Smith* (2009), and a collection of essays, *Venture Smith and the Business of Slavery and Freedom* (2010), edited by James Brewer Stewart. Vincent A. Carretta's *Phillis Wheatley: Biography of a Genius in Bondage* (2011) is a wonderful biography that provides new insights into Wheatley's life. For an examination of slavery in the revolutionary era through the eyes of an enslaved boy, see Joyce Lee Malcolm's *Peter's War: A New England Slave Boy and the American Revolution* (2009). Likewise, Denis R. Caron uses Prince Mortimer, a Connecticut freedman who died in prison, to detail the stark realities of post-emancipation life in *A Century in Captivity: The Life and Trials of Prince Mortimer, a Connecticut Slave* (2006). For individual black activists of the emancipation era, see Lamont D. Thomas's *Paul Cuffee: Black Entrepreneur and Pan-Africanist* (1988) for a biography of the mixed-race ship captain and merchant.

The literature dealing with African Americans and the American Revolution is vast, and much of it examines New England. See, for example, Douglas Egerton's *Death or Liberty: African Americans and Revolutionary America* (2009), Alan Gilbert's *Black Patriots and Loyalists: Fighting for Emancipation in the War for Independence* (2012), James W. St. G. Walker's *The Black Loyalists: The Search for a Promised Land in Nova Scotia and Sierra Leone* (1976), and Cassandra Pybus's *Epic Journeys of Freedom: Runaway Slaves of the American Revolution and Their Global Quest for Liberty* (2007). More specifically, Emily Blanck's work on the legal challenges to slavery during the era can be found in her *Tyrannicide: Forging an American Law of Slavery in Revolutionary South Carolina and Massachusetts* (2014).

There is also quite an extensive literature on social and economic change, emancipation, and the rise of racism in post-revolutionary New England. For social change that deals particularly with evangelical religion and slavery in the region, see Catherine Brekus's *Sarah Osborn's World: The Rise of Evangelical Christianity in Early America* (2013). Economic change has been extensively examined, and most of these books look at enslaved and freed people as part of that process. See Douglas Lamar Jones, *Village and Seaport: Migration and Society in Eighteenth-Century Massachusetts* (1981); Ruth Wallis Herndon, *Unwelcome Americans: Living on the Margins in Early New England*

(2001); and Cornelia H. Dayton and Sharon V. Salinger, *Robert Love's Warnings: Searching for Strangers in Colonial Boston* (2014).

Finally, the classic and still most important work on emancipation and the rise of racism in New England is Joanne Pope Melish's *Disowning Slavery: Gradual Emancipation and Race in New England, 1780–1860* (1997). Likewise, Margot Minardi's *Making Slavery History: Abolitionism and the Politics of Memory in Massachusetts* (2010) helps to make sense of how white people in New England distanced themselves from slavery and its legacies. A classic work concerning the rise of racially discriminatory laws and institutions in New England is Leon Litwack's *North of Slavery: The Negro in the Free States, 1790–1860* (1965). The best book for understanding black activism, how freed people resisted social economic change, and the emergence of the black intellectual tradition in New England is Christopher Cameron's *To Plead Our Own Cause: African Americans in Massachusetts and the Making of the Antislavery Movement* (2014).

Notes

Preface: 15 George Street, Medford, Massachusetts 02155

1. Roy E. Finkenbine, "Belinda's Petition: Reparations for Slavery in Revolutionary Massachusetts," *William and Mary Quarterly*, 3rd ser., 64, no. 1 (January 2007): 98.

Chapter 1: Origins

1. Emmanuel Downing to John Winthrop, ca. August 1645, in Allyn B. Forbes, ed., *The Winthrop Papers* (Boston: Massachusetts Historical Society, 1947), 5:38–39.
2. For more on Eaton, John and Lucretia Whan, and Jones, including the quotation, see Wendy Warren, *New England Bound: Slavery and Colonization in Early America* (New York: Liveright, 2016), 176–79.
3. Michael Guasco, *Slaves and Englishmen: Human Bondage in the Early Modern Atlantic World* (Philadelphia: University of Pennsylvania Press, 2014), 192.
4. For a discussion of Smith's vision for New England, see Neil Salisbury, *Manitou and Providence: Indians, Europeans, and the Making of New England, 1500–1643* (New York: Oxford University Press, 1982), 98–100.
5. For more on these laws, see Linford D. Fisher, "'Dangerous Designes': The 1676 Barbados Act to Prohibit New England Indian Slave Importation," *William and Mary Quarterly* 71 no. 1 (January 2014): 99–124.
6. Samuel Sewall, *The Selling of Joseph* (Boston: Bartholomew Green and John Allen, 1700), 2.
7. Boston Records Commissioners, *A Report of the Record Commissioners of the City of Boston, Containing the Boston Records from 1660 to 1701* (Boston: Rockwell and Churchill, 1881), 7:5.
8. William H. Whitmore, *The Colonial Laws of Massachusetts . . . Together with the Body of Liberties of 1641* (Boston: Rockwell and Churchill, 1890), 53.
9. For the 1652 law, see John R. Bartlett, ed., *Records of the Colony of Rhode Island and Providence Plantations, in New England* (Providence, R.I.: A. Crawford Greene and Brothers, 1856), 1:243.
10. Winthrop D. Jordan, "The Influence of the West Indies on the Origins of New England Slavery," *William and Mary Quarterly*, 3rd ser., 18, no. 2 (April 1961):

245–46. For more on this law as the possible product of a political squabble between the towns of Rhode Island, see pp. 245–46n8.

11. Lorenzo Johnston Greene, *The Negro in Colonial New England* (1942; reprint, New York: Atheneum, 1969), 126.

12. Simon P. Newman, *A New World of Labor: The Development of Plantation Slavery in the British Atlantic* (Philadelphia: University of Pennsylvania Press, 2013), 251. The classic work on the early Caribbean is Richard S. Dunn, *Sugar and Slaves: The Rise of the Planter Class in the English West Indies, 1624–1713* (Chapel Hill: University of North Carolina Press, 1972).

13. Richard Ligon, *A True and Exact History of the Island of Barbadoes* (London: Humphrey Moseley, 1657), 113.

Chapter 2: Trafficked People

1. For Byfield's description of Rose, see "Nathaniel Byfield, 1732 Will," docket no. 6391, Suffolk County Probate Records, Massachusetts State Archives, Boston. Other details about Rose can be found in Peter Benes, "Slavery in Boston Households, 1647–1770," *Annual Proceedings of the Dublin Seminar for New England Folklife* 28 (2003): 12–14.

2. Richard Dunn, James Savage, and Laetitia Yeandle, eds., *The Journal of John Winthrop* (Cambridge, MA: Harvard University Press, 1996), 246.

3. Simon Bradstreet to the Board of Trade and Plantations, 18 May 1680, in Elizabeth Donnon, ed., *Documents Illustrative of the Slave Trade*, vol. 3, *New England and the Middle Colonies* (Washington, DC: Carnegie Institution, 1932), 14–15.

4. For more on the Rhode Island slave trade, especially these figures, see Jay Coughtry, *The Notorious Triangle: Rhode Island and the African Slave Trade, 1700–1807* (Philadelphia: Temple University Press, 1981), 26.

5. An account of the *Little George* can be found in the *Boston News-Letter*, 6 May 1731.

6. For the story of Mary Bowen and more on the widespread investment in slavery in Rhode Island, see Rachel Chernos Lin, "The Rhode Island Slave-Traders: Butchers, Bakers, and Candlestick-Makers," *Slavery and Abolition* 23, no. 3 (2002): 33.

7. Peter Faneuil to Peter Buckley, 3 February 1738, in *Proceedings of the Massachusetts Historical Society*, 1st ser., 7 (1864): 418.

8. Hugh Hall Account Book, 1728–33, pp. 6 (shipping slaves), 28–30 (list of imported slaves from Barbados), Hugh Hall Papers, box 1, Ms. N-1352, Massachusetts Historical Society, Boston.

9. Paul J. Lindholdt, ed., *John Josselyn, Colonial Traveler: A Critical Edition of Two Voyages to New-England* (Hanover, NH: University Press of New England, 1988), 24.

10. Ibid., 142.

11. For more on the "queen," west central Africa, Atlantic creoles, and how she most likely ended up in New England, see John K. Thornton and Linda M.

Heywood, "'Canniball Negroes,' Atlantic Creoles, and the Identity of New England's Charter Generation," *African Diaspora* 4 (2011): 89–94.

12. *Boston News-Letter,* 22 July 1717.

13. More information on Carolina Indians in New England and all the quotations in this section can be found in Margaret Ellen Newell, *Brethren by Nature: New England Indians, Colonists, and the Origins of American Slavery* (Ithaca, NY: Cornell University Press, 2015), 204–10.

14. *The Last and Dying Words of Mark, Aged about 30 Years* (Boston, 1755).

15. For Smith's narrative, see *A Narrative of the Life and Adventures of Venture, a Native of Africa: But Resident above Sixty Years in the United States of America. Related by Himself* (New London, CT: C. Holt, 1798).

Chapter 3: Slave and Society

1. For more on Onesimus and Mather, see Kathryn S. Koo, "Strangers in the House of God: Cotton Mather, Onesimus, and an Experiment in Christian Slaveholding," *Proceedings of the American Antiquarian Society* 17, no. 1 (2007): 143–75.

2. Gordon S. Wood, *The Radicalism of the American Revolution* (New York: Knopf, 1991), 19.

3. Quoted in Carl Bridenbaugh, *Cities in Revolt: Urban Life in America* (New York: Oxford University Press, 1971), 137.

4. Robert Olwell has explored patriarchy as it relates to slavery and the social order. For the quotations here, see Robert Olwell, *Masters, Slaves, and Subjects: The Culture of Power in the South Carolina Low Country, 1740–1790* (Ithaca, NY: Cornell University Press, 1998), 191–92. The passage on the universe can be found in Soame Jenyns, *A Free Inquiry into the Nature and Origin of Evil* (London, 1757), quoted in ibid., 192.

5. William Blackstone, *Commentaries on the Laws of England* (Oxford: Clarendon, 1769), 4:127.

6. Benjamin Franklin, *The Autobiography of Benjamin Franklin* (Mineola, NY: Dover, 1996), 15.

7. Samuel Sewall, *The Selling of Joseph: A Memorial* (Boston: B. Green and John Allen, 1700), 2.

8. John Saffin, *A Brief and Candid Answer to a Late Printed Sheet, Entituled, The Selling of Joseph* (Boston, 1700), reprinted in Louis Ruchames, ed., *Racial Thought in America: A Documentary History,* vol. 1, *From the Puritans to Abraham Lincoln* (Amherst: University of Massachusetts Press, 1969), 56–57.

9. For MacSparran's diary, see James MacSparran, *Abstract and Letterbook of Out Services,* ed. Wilkins Updike (Boston: Merrymount Press, 1899), 24, 27 (quotations).

10. Vincent Caretta, *Phillis Wheatley: Biography of a Genius in Bondage* (Athens: University of Georgia Press, 2011), 14–23.

11. For the case, see "Case of Jeffs (Negro) and Parthenia (Negro), Slaves of Mary

Minott," n.d., Suffolk Files no. 101791, Massachusetts State Archives, Boston (hereafter MSA).

12. "Case of Toney, a Negroman of Samuel Johnson," June 1756, Suffolk Files no. 75761, MSA.

13. "Deposition of Sarah Bartlett," 1 September 1735, Suffolk Files no. 166505, MSA.

14. "Examination of Nanny, Negro Servant to Capt. Joseph Hinkley," 5 November 1745, Suffolk Files no. 61232, MSA.

15. "Otis and Hinckley," July 1746, Suffolk Files no. 62026, MSA.

16. Lorenzo Johnston Greene, *The Negro in Colonial New England* (1942: reprint, New York: Atheneum, 1969), 170–71.

17. John Russell Bartlett, *Records of the Colony of Rhode Island and Providence Plantation in New England*, vol. 5, *1741 to 1756* (Providence, RI: Knowles, Anthony, 1860), 72–73. For more on Cuff and Taylor, see Elaine Forman Crane, *Witches, Wife Beaters, and Whores: Common Law and Common Folk in Early America* (Ithaca, NY: Cornell University Press, 2011), chap. 4.

18. The story of Lucy and Mathias Plant can be found in Dinah Mayo-Bobee, "Servile Discontents: Slavery and Resistance in Colonial New Hampshire, 1645–1785," *Slavery and Abolition* 30, no. 3 (September 2009): 347.

19. The Rhode Island Historical Society holds Cesar Lyndon's diary. See Cesar Lyndon, "Journal," Rhode Island Manuscripts, 10:81–85, Rhode Island Historical Society, Providence.

20. For an account of the murder of Codman and Revere's quotation, see Abner Cheney Goodall, *The Trial and Execution, for Petit Treason, of Mark and Phillis* (Cambridge, MA: John Wilson and Son, 1883), 30.

21. *Boston News Letter*, 14 April 1738.

Chapter 4: Working Worlds

1. *Boston Gazette*, 22 January 1754.

2. Venture Smith, *A Narrative of the Life and Adventures of Venture, a Native of Africa: But Resident above Sixty Years in the United States of America. Related by Himself* (New London, CT: C. Holt, 1798), 23.

3. Trevor Burnard, *Mastery, Tyranny, and Desire: Thomas Thistlewood and His Slaves in the Anglo-Jamaican World* (Chapel Hill: University of North Carolina Press, 2004), 55–58.

4. For Spear's "memoir," see A Lady of Boston [Rebecca Warren Brown], *Memoir of Mrs. Chloe Spear, a Native of Africa, Who Was Enslaved in Childhood and Died in Boston January 3, 1815 . . . Aged 65 Years* (Boston: James Loring, 1832), 32–33. Details of her later life can be found in Margot Minardi, *Making Slavery History: Abolitionism and the Politics of Memory in Massachusetts* (Cambridge, MA: Harvard University Press, 2010), 112–13.

5. Oxenbridge Thatcher, Will, 1772, docket no. 15261, Suffolk County Probate Records, Massachusetts State Archives, Boston; Mary Guillion, Indenture, 1753, Overseer of the Poor Taking Books, 2:28, Boston Public Library (hereafter BPL).

6. Boston Records Commissioners, *A Report of the Record Commissioners of Boston:*

Records Relating to the Early History of Boston (Boston: Rockwell and Churchill, 1883), 8:225.

7. Jared Sparks, ed., "Bennett's History of New England," *Proceedings of the Massachusetts Historical Society*, 1st ser., 5 (1860–62): 124–25.

8. For the Eustis accounts, see Boston Town Records, MS.f.BOS.7 vol. 2, BPL. The schoolhouse project can be found on p. 144 and the other jobs are on p. 151.

9. *Boston Evening-Post*, 19 December 1748.

10. *Boston Evening-Post*, 25 August 1735.

11. Isaiah Thomas, *The History of Printing in America, with a Biography of Printers*, 2nd edition (1808; New York: Burt Franklin, 1874), 1:99.

12. Indenture, 12 October 1760, recorded 9 August 1769, Ezekiel Price Notary Records, vol. 5, Boston Athenæum.

13. Briton Hammon, *A Narrative of the Uncommon Sufferings and Surprizing Deliverance of Briton Hammon* (Boston: Green and Russell, 1760).

14. For Jackson and his working world, see Allegra di Bonaventura, *For Adam's Sake: A Family Saga in Colonial New England* (New York: Liveright, 2013), 289–302, 299 (quotation).

15. George Sheldon, *A History of Deerfield, Massachusetts* (Deerfield, MA: Pocumtuck Valley Memorial Association, 1896), 2:897.

16. Parkman kept extensive diaries for his entire life, but they have been published in bits and pieces. For the material regarding the slave sale at Elias Parkman's house and concerning Maro's death, see Harriette M. Forbes, *The Diary of Ebenezer Parkman of Westborough, Mass.* (Westborough, MA: Westborough Historical Society, 1899), vi. The material on Maro and his work can be found in Francis G. Walett, "The Diary of Ebenezer Parkman, 1719–1728," *Proceedings of the American Antiquarian Society* 71 (April 1961): 129–31.

17. Quoted in Wilkins Updike, *A History of the Episcopal Church in Narragansett, Rhode Island* (New York: Henry M. Onderdonk, 1847), 181.

Chapter 5: Kin and Community

1. For more on the collision of African customs of marriage with New England practices, see William D. Piersen, *Black Yankees: The Development of an Afro-American Subculture in Eighteenth-Century New England* (Amherst: University of Massachusetts Press, 1988), 87–88.

2. Quoted in Marjory Gomez O'Toole, *If Jane Should Want to Be Sold: Stories of Enslavement, Indenture, and Freedom in Little Compton, Rhode Island* (Little Compton, RI: Little Compton Historical Society, 2016), 130.

3. The 1754 census returns can be found in Lorenzo J. Greene, *The Negro in Colonial New England, 1620–1776* (New York: Columbia University Press, 1942), appendix C.

4. "Deposition of James and Sarah Gardiner, Case of Quaco (Negro)," 13 September 1762, Suffolk Files no. 83313, Massachusetts State Archives, Boston (hereafter MSA).

5. Nathaniel Bouton, *The History of Concord, from Its First Grant in 1725* (Concord, NH: Benning W. Sanborn, 1856), 252.

6. Samuel Phillips, "A Form for a *Negroe-Marriage*," in George H. Moore, "Slave Marriages in Massachusetts," *Historical Magazine* 5 (1869): 137.

7. Robert H. Romer, *Slavery in the Connecticut River Valley of Massachusetts* (Florence, MA: Levellers Press, 2009), 148.

8. The story of Jinny and Cato can be found in George Sheldon, *The History of Deerfield, Massachusetts* (Deerfield, MA: Pocumtuck Valley Memorial Association, 1896), 2:896–98.

9. *Boston News-Letter*, 26 June 1760.

10. The account of Silvia and Hagar can be found in Piersen, *Black Yankees*, 94.

11. Quoted in Oliver P. Fuller, *The History of Warwick, Rhode Island* (Providence, RI: Angell, Burlingame, 1875), 189.

12. Quoted in Jared Ross Hardesty, *Unfreedom: Slavery and Dependence in Eighteenth-Century Boston* (New York: New York University Press, 2016), 99.

13. *Boston Post-Boy*, 14 September 1741.

14. *Boston Evening Post*, 14 January 1740.

15. For more on Quash, especially this episode, see Diane Cameron, "Enslavement, Freedom, Possibility, and Poverty: Four Generations of Quash Gomer's Family in Connecticut, 1748–1874," *Annual Proceedings of the Dublin Seminar for New England Folklife* 28 (2003): 106.

16. John Winthrop, *Winthrop's Journal: History of New England, 1630–1649*, ed. James Kendall Hosmer (New York: Charles Scribner's Sons, 1908), 2:26.

17. Lorenzo Greene offers some of these figures. See Greene, *Negro in Colonial New England*, 268. The most comprehensive account of the number of enslaved people in New England parishes comes from Richard Boles, "Dividing the Faith: The Rise of Racially Segregated Northern Churches, 1730–1850" (Ph.D. diss., George Washington University, 2013).

18. Vincent Carretta, *Phillis Wheatley: Biography of a Genius in Bondage* (Athens: University of Georgia Press, 2011), 61.

19. "Dr. Timothy Cutler to the Secretary," 11 December 1740, in William Stevens Perry, ed., *Papers Relating to the History of Church in Massachusetts, A.D. 1676–1785* (N.p., 1873), 348.

20. Boston Records Commissioners, *A Report of the Record Commissioners of the City of Boston, Containing the Records of Boston Selectmen, 1716 to 1736* (Boston: Rockwell and Churchill, 1885), 13:283.

21. *Boston Post-Boy*, 25 January 1748.

22. *Boston Post-Boy*, 23 July 1750. For more on Pompey and Goodwin, see Patricia Q. Wall, *Lives of Consequence: Blacks in Early Kittery and Berwick in the Massachusetts Province of Maine* (Portsmouth, NH: Portsmouth Marine Society, 2017), 61, 64–65.

23. Barney's case is the subject of a long entry in Daniel Allen Hearn, *Legal Executions in New England: A Comprehensive Reference, 1623–1960* (Jefferson, NC: McFarland, 1999), 135, 136. Lorenzo Greene also discusses the case in *Negro in Colonial New England*, 155–56. For the special legislative act, see Charles J.

Hoadly, *The Public Records of the Colony of Connecticut, 1636–1776* (Hartford: Case, Lockwood, and Brainard, 1874), 578–79.

24. *Boston Evening Post,* 22 February 1773.

25. The story of Phillis and the poisoning can be found across legal records and newspapers. See "Case of Phillis, Negro Servant of John Greenleaf," February 1751, Suffolk Files no. 67676, MSA; *Boston Post-Boy,* 21 January 1751; *Boston Evening Post,* 21 January, 4 March, 22 April, 20 May 1751; and Hearn, *Legal Executions,* 140.

26. "Case of William Healy and Robin (Servant of Henry Vassall)," May 1752, Suffolk Files no. 69278, MSA.

27. Very few historians have written about the 1723 conspiracy. The original trial documents are held at the Massachusetts State Archive. For Diego, see "Testimony of Diego Negro," 10 April 1723, Suffolk Files no. 16899, MSA.

28. *New England Weekly Journal,* 6 October 1741. More information on "Spanish Negroes" can be found in Charles R. Foy, "Ports of Slavery, Ports of Freedom: How Slaves Used Northern Seaports' Maritime Industry to Escape and Create Trans-Atlantic Identities" (Ph.D. diss., Rutgers University, 2008), chap. 4.

29. Natalie Zemon Davis, "Judges, Masters, Diviners: Slaves' Experience of Criminal Justice in Colonial Suriname," *Law and History Review* 29, no. 4 (November 2011): 960.

Chapter 6: Revolution and Emancipation

1. James Otis, *The Rights of the British Colonies Asserted and Proved* (Boston: Edes and Gill, 1764), 29.

2. For more on Hopkins, Osborn, and slavery, see Catherine A. Brekus, *Sarah Osborn's World: The Rise of Evangelical Christianity in Early America* (New Haven, CT: Yale University Press, 2013), 281–88, 287 (quotation).

3. Manumission, 17 August 1768, Ezekiel Price Notarial Records, vol. 4, Boston Athenæum.

4. Manumission, 19 October 1779, Ezekiel Price Notarial Records, vol. 6, Boston Athenæum.

5. For more on the recession of the 1760s, see Gary B. Nash, *The Urban Crucible: Social Change, Political Consciousness, and the Origins of the American Revolution* (Cambridge, MA: Harvard University Press, 1979), chap. 9.

6. Phillis Wheatley, "On Being Brought from Africa to America," in *Complete Writings,* ed. Vincent Carretta (New York: Penguin, 2001), 13.

7. For the January 1773 petition, see "Slave Petition for Freedom," 6 January 1773, in Herbert Aptheker, ed., *A Documentary History of the Negro People in the United States* (New York: Citadel, 1960), 1:6–7.

8. See "Peter Bestes and Other Slaves Petition for Freedom," 20 April 1773, in Aptheker, ed., *Documentary History of the Negro People,* 7–8.

9. "Petition of a Great Number of Negroes," *Massachusetts Historical Society Collections,* 3rd ser., 3 (1877): 436.

10. Abigail Adams to John Adams, 22 September 1774, in L. H. Butterfield et al.,

eds., *Adams Family Correspondence*, vol. 1, *December 1761–May 1776* (Cambridge, MA: Belknap Press of Harvard University Press, 1963), 1:161–62.

11. For the petitions to Gage, see "Negro Petitions for Freedom," *Massachusetts Historical Society Collections*, 5th ser., 3 (1877): 432–35.

12. For more on Rhode Island and the First, see Christy Clark-Pujara, *Dark Work: The Business of Slavery in Rhode Island* (New York: New York University Press, 2016), 78–79.

13. Ibid.

14. Douglas R. Egerton, *Death or Liberty: African Americans and Revolutionary America* (New York: Oxford University Press, 2009), 95.

15. Jacobs, Primus (Colored), Dinah, Record no. W.21446, Massachusetts, Revolutionary War Pension Records, National Archives and Records Administration, Washington, DC.

16. Samuel Tucker to "Mr. Barron," 17 January 1778, Commodore Tucker Papers, vol. 1, Houghton Library, Harvard University, Cambridge, MA.

17. Figures from the database based on "Book of Negroes, 1783," Carleton Papers, Library and Archives Canada, http://www.bac-lac.gc.ca.

18. *Boston Evening Post*, 6 June 1774.

19. This information can be extrapolated from the Book of Negroes. Alexander Robertson, Pompey's employer, sponsored his emigration. For an image of this page of the book, see "Book of Negroes," http://www.blackloyalist.info.

20. Documents do show that there was a printing press "in constant operation" by 1794, and it most likely belonged to Pompey Fleet. See James W. St. G. Walker, *The Black Loyalists: The Search for a Promised Land in Nova Scotia and Sierra Leone, 1783–1870* (Toronto: University of Toronto Press, 1992), 204.

21. For the clause in the constitution of 1777, see Harvey Amani Whitfield, *The Problem of Slavery in Early Vermont, 1777–1810* (Barre: Vermont Historical Society, 2014), 57.

22. For a discussion of the gradual emancipation bills in Connecticut and Rhode Island, and the political machinations around them, see Joanne Pope Melish, *Disowning Slavery: Gradual Emancipation and "Race" in New England, 1780–1860* (Ithaca, NY: Cornell University Press, 1997), 67–69.

23. Clark-Pujara, *Dark Work*, 80–81.

24. Theodore Sedgwick's daughter, famed novelist Catharine Maria Sedgwick, grew up with Elizabeth Freeman as her caretaker and later left an account of her life. See Catharine Maria Sedgwick, "Slavery in New England," in *Bentley's Miscellany* (London: Richard Bentley, 1853), 34:417–24, 418, 421 (quotations).

25. Jeremy Belknap, "Queries Relating to Slavery in Massachusetts," *Massachusetts Historical Society Collections*, 3rd ser., 3 (1877): 386.

26. David Waldstreicher, *Slavery's Constitution: From Revolution to Ratification* (New York: Hill and Wang, 2009), 154–56.

Epilogue: The Problems of Emancipation

1. John Adams to Jeremy Belknap, 21 March 1795, in "Letters and Documents Relating to Slavery in Massachusetts," *Massachusetts Historical Society Collections,* 5th ser., 3 (1877), 402.

2. William Cooper Nell recounted this story in his *The Colored Patriots of the American Revolution, with Sketches of Several Distinguished Colored Person* (Boston: Robert F. Wallcut, 1855), 59–60.

3. Quoted in John Wood Sweet, *Bodies Politic: Negotiating Race in the American North, 1730–1830* (Philadelphia: University of Pennsylvania Press, 2006), 260–61.

4. Philip Slead to Moses Brown, 26 December 1793, Moses Brown Papers, Rhode Island Historical Society, Providence.

5. Petition of Prince Hall to the Massachusetts General Court, 27 February 1788, Jeremy Belknap Papers, Massachusetts Historical Society, Boston.

6. Manumission, 25 February 1789, Ezekiel Price Notary Books, vol. 7, Boston Athenæum.

7. Cato Freeman's story can be found in Ruth Herndon, *Unwelcome Americans: Living on the Margins in Early New England* (Philadelphia: University of Pennsylvania Press, 2001), 100–103.

8. Manumission, 2 February 1770, Ezekiel Price Notary Books, vol. 5, Boston Athenæum.

9. Quoted in Joanne Pope Melish, *Disowning Slavery: Gradual Emancipation and "Race" in New England, 1780–1860* (Ithaca, NY: Cornell University Press, 1997), 106.

10. "An Act to Prevent the Sale and Transportation of Negroes and Molattoes Out of This State" (1786), in Harvey Amani Whitfield, ed., *The Problem of Slavery in Early Vermont, 1777–1810* (Barre: Vermont Historical Society, 2014), 74.

Index

Page numbers in italics indicate figures.

abolition: petitions for, 126–28; of slave trade, 136–37

abolitionism, 119–34, 139, 143–44, 146, 148; American Revolution and, 134–35, 138; antislavery arguments and, 54–55, 119–20, 141; antislavery legislation and, 14–15; black activism for, 122–28, 138–46, 153; black intellectual tradition and, 122–28; colonization and, 127–28; religious motives for, 120–21, 126, 153; sectionalism and, 151–53

Adams, John, 129, 138–39, 146

advertisements: for fugitives from slavery, 38–39, 70, 102, 110–12, 133, 151; for hiring out slaves, 70, 72, *73*; for selling enslaved people, 64, 70, 99

African Lodge No. 1, 137–38

Africans, perception of difference by English, 2, 4–6, 11, 53, 144

African slavery: in Caribbean, 12, 44; in New England, 33–34, 48, 86, 91, 95, 102; New England merchants' involvement in, 20–22, 26–34, 38, 47–48, 81; transition from Indian enslavement to, 11–12, 34, 41

Anglicans, 8–9, 34

antislavery. *See* abolitionism

apprenticeship, 3, 45, 52–54, 60, 79, 84, 135

arson, as form of resistance, 113, 115

artisans, 71–76, 79–80, 123, 146

Atlantic creoles. *See* creoles

Baptists, 9, 15

Barbados, 12, 16, 18–23, 32, *33*, 43–44, 47

Bible, justifications of slavery found in, 4–5, 12–14, 16, 23, 49, 63

bondsmen and -women. *See* enslaved people

Book of Negroes, 133

Boston, xiii–xv, 13, 31, *33*, 34, 48, 60, 68, 71, 76–82, 108, 110, 115–16, 129, 133–34

Brom and Bett v. Ashley, 139

Brown University, 120

Canada, slaves sold to, 147–48

capital punishment, 41–44, 60, 64–66, 101, 113, 115

Caribbean: black slaves sold from New England to, 147–48; economic connections to New England, 2, 12–13, 17, 21–23, 26, 28–29, 31–32, 81, 91, 120, 122; Indian captives traded in, xvi, 2, 11–12, 17, 23–27; social connections to New England, xvi, 22, 32

Carolinas, Indian slave trade in, 38–41

child labor, 11, 52, 71, 146

children: "binding out" of, 3, 52, 54, 60, 78; enslaved, 27, 31, 43, 47, 79; of enslaved people, 15–16, 22–23, 54–55, 57, 94, 98–102, 117, 122, 135–36

Christianity: in Africa, 36, 38, 106; conversion of enslaved people to, 12, 25, 49–50, 60, 105–6, 123–26; Indians and, 2, 11–12

churches, enslaved people and, 94–95, 105–6, 109–10

civic celebrations, slaves participating in, 107–9, 128, 141–42
Codman, John, 41, 43, 66, 72
colonization, 128, 134, 146
Commonwealth v. Jennison, 140, 151. *See also* freedom suits
commodities, 4–5, 10, 17–22, 26–28, 37–40, 81–82, 91, 152
Connecticut: enslaved labor in, 34, *58*, 87–88; gradual emancipation in, 135–37, 140–41; regulation of slavery in, 66–68
conspiracies, 41, 104, 113–16, 128–29
Continental Army, black soldiers in, 131–33, 149
conversion, of Indians and Africans, 11–12, 25, 36, 49–50, 60, 105–6, 123, 126, 144
Copley, John Singleton, 113, *114*
corporal punishment, 52–53, 55, 60, 66–67, 101, 111–12
courtship, 95–97
creoles, 38, 43–44, 48
criminal servitude, 11
Cuffee, Paul, 123, 146, 150
curfews, 67–69, 96, 103–4

debt peonage, 11
Declaration of Independence, 128, 134
Deerfield, Massachusetts, 48, 86, 88–89, 98
dependence, 3, 50–57, 69, 150
distilling, 28, 70–71, 81–82. *See also* rum
domestic labor, enslaved women and, xiv, 13, *58*, 71–72, 76–78, 89. *See also* family; household labor
Downing, Emmanuel, 1–2, 10–12, 17

emancipation: black activism for, 119, 122–29, 134, 137–41; in Connecticut, 136; gradual, 135–37, 143, 150; judicial, in Massachusetts, 137–40, 150–51; military service in exchange for, 130, 132–33; racism and, 144–47, 150; religious arguments for, 9, 120–21, 126; in Rhode Island, 136–37; in Vermont, 134–35, 151. *See also* abolition; manumission; natural rights discourse; petitions
England, slavery and, 2–3, 6, 23, 27, 127
English Civil War, 10, 19
Enlightenment, 124
enslaved people: as consumers, xvii, 75, 78; cultural traditions of, xvii, 36–38, 72, 94–95, 97–100, 107–9, 116; importance

to New England economy of, xv–xvi, 12, 27–29, 70, 74; legally ambiguous status of, 64; proportion of population in New England, xv, 2, 33, 34, 76, 141; regulation of social lives of, 67, 103; religion and, 25, 36, 99; status of children of, 15, 22, 54, 122; as status symbols, 79
evangelicalism, 106–7, 120

family: in Africa, 43, 44, 46; enslaved, 26, 72, 93–102, 117, 149; labor and, 7, 71, 72; merchant connections to Caribbean, xiii–xv, 17, 22, 32; slaves as part of masters', 50–51, 53, 56–60. *See also* domestic labor; household labor
family slavery, 57–58
Faneuil, Peter, 31
fishing industry, 10, 17, 21–23, 35, 72
food crops, 10, 18–19, 21–22
Franklin, Benjamin, 53
free black people, 54, 101, 108, 117, 122–31, 137–41, 145–46, 148–49
freedom suits, 138–40
free labor, ideology of, 3, 143
Freemasonry, 137–38
funerals, of black new Englanders, 107–8

Gage, Thomas, 129, 133
gender ratios, xvii, 95–96
gender: labor and, 71–72, 86; punishment and, 65
Glorious Revolution, 28, 105

Hall, Hugh, Jr., 32–33
Hall, Prince, xv, 137, 147–48
Hammon, Briton, 84–85
Hancock, John, 124, 147
Hazard, Robert, 91, 152–53
Hazard, Rowland, 152–53
hierarchy, 50–54, 69
Holbrook, Felix, 126–27
household labor, 13, 56–58, 70–71, 76–77, 91
households, 56–58, 60–62
Hutchinson, Thomas, 124

Imperial Crisis, 118–30
indentured servitude, 5, 19, 34, 84, 91, 135–36, 147–48, 151
Indian captives, trafficking of, 1, 11–12, 14, 17, 20–21, 23, 26, 38–39

Indian enslavement: laws regarding, 11–12, 16, 39–41, 65–66, 130; in New England, 6, 11–12, 16, 34
Indians: Christian, 11–12; imported to New England from Carolinas, 38–41; intermarriage with Africans, 101–2, 122–23, 133; intermarriage with whites, 101; marriage, 94–95, 117; racialization of, 8, 14, 16, 53, 66–68
Indians, wars with, 1–2, 11–12, 16, 39–40, 60

Jackson, Adam (slave of Joshua Hempstead), 86–88
Jamaica, 12, 22, 116
Josselyn, John, 9, 34–38
judicial emancipation, in Massachusetts, 137–40, 150–51

King Philip's War, 12, 102
Kongo, 26, 36–37, 98

labor: agricultural, 70, 86–87, 90–91; domestic, 13, 58, 76, 78–79, 88–89; enslaved Indian, 11, 21; gendered, 71, 86; industrial, enslaved workers in, 5, 71, 76, 79, 81; maritime, 76, 81–82, 84–85, 102; rural, 12, 71–72, 86–91; skilled, enslaved workers in, 13, 40, 44, 70, 72, 79, 82; theories of, 3, 8; urban, 71–72, 76–85
labor market, free blacks in, after emancipation, 144, 146–47
labor shortages: in the Caribbean, 17, 19–20; in England, 3; in New England, 1, 2, 10, 11, 92, 119
laws, New England regulation of slavery in, 13–16, 22–23, 33–34, 41, 62–69
literacy, 25, 41, 49, 58, 65, 106, 119, 123
Little George, 29–30
livestock production, 86–87, 91, 113, 152. *See also* commodities
loyalists, 133–34

MacSparran, James, 55–57
Maine, 8–9, 35–36, 60, 92, 111, *112*
manumission, 68, 78, 121–23, 136, 138, 149
Mark (slave of Codman), 41–43, 66, 72
Maro (slave of Parkman), 89–90
Maroca (slave of MacSparran), 55, 57
marriage: enslaved, 68, 94–98, 100; interracial, 67–68, 101–2
Massachusetts: abolition in, 138–40, 151;

laws regulating slavery in, 13–14, 33, 63, 67–69, 94–95
Mather, Cotton, 49–50, 105
Maverick, Samuel, 9, 35–38
ministers, 49–50, 75, 88–89, 95, 105
molasses. *See* commodities
Mumford, Thomas, 46–47
murder, 41, 60, 65–66, 96

Nanny (slave of Joseph Hinkley), 61–62
Narragansett Country, 71, 86, 90–91
Narragansett Indians, 1, 11, 17
natural-rights discourse, 119, 121, 124, 128–29, 138
Negro Election Day, 108–9
New Brunswick, 147
New London, Connecticut, 86–87
Newport, Rhode Island, 15, 29, 34, 76, 81, 107
New York, slave conspiracies in, 41, 115
Nova Scotia, 48, 134, 147

Onesimus (slave of Mather), 49–50
Osborn, Sarah, 107, 120

Parkman, Ebenezer, 89–90
paternalism, 56, 135
patriarchy, 49–58, 60, 69
pauper apprenticeship, 52, 60, 78
Pequot War, 11, 20, 26
personhood, legal ambiguity of slaves', 63–65
petitions, xv, 123, 126–29, 147–48, 150
piracy, 9, 27
pirates: *See* privateers
Plymouth, 71, 81
Plymouth Colony, 6–8, 11
Poems on Various Subjects, Religious and Moral (Wheatley), 124, *125*
poisoning, 41, 96; as form of resistance, 113, 116
polygamy, 94, 100
poor relief. *See* pauper apprenticeship
poor whites, 145–47, 149, 152
port towns, 12, 28, 31, 59, 71, 76, 80, 82, 87, 94–95, 123
Portuguese, xvi, 18, 26, 36–38
poverty, 52, 104, 135, 144, 149–50, 152
pregnancy, 57, 61–62
print culture, 5, 38, 82, 110, 121, 123–24, 133–34, 145

privateers, 5–6, 17–18, 37–38, 116
property, enslaved people as, 44, 62–64, 75, 95, 97–99, 135, 147
property ownership: slaves and, 65, 126; free blacks and, 102, 149, 150
protest movements, and American Revolution, 118–19, 122, 141
Providence, Rhode Island, 13, 15, 120–21, 141, 149
Providence Abolition Society, 148
Providence Island, 11, 20, 26, 38
Providence Society for Abolishing the Slave Trade, 121
public events, enslaved people's participation in, 93, 107–9, 128
public works, enslaved people working on, 79–81

Quakers, 9, 15, 120–21, 153
"Queen" (slave of Maverick), 35–38

race, 67, 69, 119, 138, 141
racism, 6, 53, 118, 126, 144; after emancipation, 144–47, 150–53
resistance, 29, 41, 60, 109–17
Rhode Island: abolitionists in, 120–21; gradual emancipation in, 135; legislation about slavery in, 14–15, 41, 67–68, 147–48; slavery in, 9, 15, 34, 64, 76, 90–91, 141; slave trade and, 29–30, 48, 81, 91, 136–37
Rhode Island First Battalion, 130–31
Rights of the British Colonies Asserted and Proved, The (James Otis), 119
Royal African Company, 27–28
Royal American Gazette, 134
Royall family, xiii–xv
rum, xiv, 28, 46, 48, 81
runaway slave advertisements, 38, 102, 110–12, 116, 133, 151. See also self-emancipation
rural slavery, 86–92

sailors. See labor: maritime
Salem, Massachusetts, 13, 26, 59, 61, 71, 81, 95, 105, 132
segregation, 68, 118, 130, 143, 153, 146
self-emancipation, 38, 40–41, 60, 67, 70, 93, 96, 109–11, 117, 133, 140, 151
self-hire, 73–75, 92
self-purchase, 75, 122–23

Selling of Joseph, The (Sewall), 54
servitude, inheritable, 15–16, 23
Seven Years' War, 123, 138
Sewall, Samuel, 12, 54–55, 68
sexual violence, 35–36, 61–62, 64, 67, 69, 100–101
shipbuilding, xv, 10, 70–71, 81, 87
slave codes, 16–17, 23, 63, 66–68
slave rebellions, 29–30, 40–41, 115–17
slavery, global, xvi, 2–6, 23. See also African slavery
slavery, regulation of in New England, 62–63. See also abolition; enslaved people; labor; manumission
slaves. See enslaved people
slave trade: African, 27–28, 45–46; regulation in New England of, 32–33, 41; restrictions on after independence, 136–37; transatlantic, 15, 31–32, 46, 48, 51
Smith, John, 6, 11
Smith, Venture, 44–47, 73–76, 150
smuggling, 9, 27, 127
social order. See hierarchy
Somerset v. Stewart, 126–27
South Carolina, 23, 40, 63, 90
Spain, 5–6, 37, 39, 84–85, 116
Spear, Chloe (slave of John Bradford), 77–78
strangers, 3–4, 8, 12–14, 20, 54
sugar. See commodities
surveillance, 57, 66–68
Sutton, Belinda, xiv–xv

Tacky's Revolt, 116
taverns, 103–4
taxation, of enslaved people as property, 63–64, 95
theft, as resistance by enslaved people, 114–15
timber. See commodities
tobacco. See commodities
Tuscarora War, 40

urban slavery, 76–85

Vermont, abolition of slavery in, 134–35, 151
violence: against enslaved people, 52–57, 60–62, 111; resistance by enslaved people and, 111–12
Virginia, 10, 16–17, 23, 29, 63, 90

wage labor, 59, 72–75, 84, 87, 92, 103–4, 122
war captives, trafficking of, 1–2, 11–16, 20, 23, 26, 37–40, 45–46, 116
War of Independence, 130–34; black loyalists in, 133–134; black patriots in, 130–32, 149
War of Spanish Succession, 39–40
wars, Indian. *See* King Philip's War; Pequot War
Washington, George, 131
West Indies. *See* Caribbean

Wheatley, Phillis, 57–58, 106, 124–26
Whitefield, George, 107
widows, 59, 132
Williams, Roger, 9, 15
Winthrop, John, 1–2, 26–28, 105
women: free black, xiv–xv, 101, 135, 149; Indian, 102, 117, 122–23
women, enslaved: children of, 15, 54, 98–100, 135; marriage and, 94–98, 100–101; sexual violence and, 34–38, 57–59, 61–62

JARED ROSS HARDESTY is associate professor of history at Western Washington University. He received his PhD from Boston College in 2014 and is a scholar of colonial America, the Atlantic world, and the histories of labor and slavery. Hardesty is the author of *Unfreedom: Slavery and Dependence in Eighteenth-Century Boston* (NYU Press, 2016) and numerous articles and book reviews. He lives in Bellingham, Washington, with his wife, Dana.